Twayne's Filmmakers Series

Warren French
EDITOR

John Huston

John Huston on the set of Annie. *Courtesy of Movie Star News.*

John Huston

SCOTT HAMMEN

BOSTON

Twayne Publishers

1985

John Huston

is first published in 1985 by Twayne Publishers,
A Division of G. K. Hall & Company
All Rights Reserved

Copyright © 1985 by G. K. Hall & Co.

Book Production by Elizabeth Todesco

Printed on permanent/durable acid-free paper and bound
in the United States of America.

First Printing, 1985

Library of Congress in Publication Data

Hammen, Scott.
John Huston

(Twayne's filmmakers series)
Bibliography: p. 144
Filmography: p. 146
Includes index.
1. Huston, John, 1906–
—Criticism and interpretation.
I. Title.   II. Series.
PN1998.A3H79   1985   791.43'0233'0924   85-8471
ISBN 0-8057-9299-6

Contents

About the Author

SCOTT HAMMEN WAS BORN in Chicago. He graduated from Amherst College with a B.A., then received an M.F.A. from the Visual Studies Workshop, State University of New York at Buffalo in 1975. Until 1981, he was an adjunct assistant professor at the University of Louisville, where he organized film programs at the J. B. Speed Art Museum. The museum published two collections of program notes that he had researched at the Museum of Modern Art Film Study Center. He now lives in Paris and works on his own films.

Editor's Foreword

ON 3 MARCH 1983 the American Film Institute presented its eleventh annual Life Achievement Award to John Huston. He was the sixth director to be so honored. The first award, in 1973, was presented to John Ford; subsequent presentations were made to Orson Welles (1973), William Wyler (1976), Alfred Hitchcock (1979), and Frank Capra (1982). Three of the half dozen began their American directing careers in the now legendary years of 1940–41 at the very top of the heap, each directing one of his greatest achievements and a classic of the American film repertoire—Hitchcock's *Rebecca*, Welles's *Citizen Kane*, and Huston's *The Maltese Falcon*.

Although Huston's career was interrupted after only three films by four years in uniform making controversial documentaries for the United States Army Signal Corps during World War II, he reestablished himself as a top-rank filmmaker with another of his greatest successes, *The Treasure of the Sierra Madre* in 1948. Although his career had ups and downs over the next thirty-five years, he never encountered the kinds of problems that plagued the temperamental Welles, many of whose works fell into obscurity or went unrealized (including the unfinished *The Other Side of the Wind*, in which John Huston played the leading role).

Breaking away from Hollywood and establishing the now fashionable practice of shooting films in exotic places around the world, Huston turned out another thirty commercial films, including such frequently revived classics as *The Asphalt Jungle*, *The African Queen*, *Moulin Rouge*, *The Misfits*, and *The Man Who Would Be King*, by the time he received the AFI award. He showed also an unusual gift for adapting great novels to the screen in such still underappreciated productions as *The Red Badge of Courage*, *Moby Dick*, *Reflections in a Golden Eye*, and *Wise Blood*. Although he at times relaxed with frivolous films like *Beat the Devil* and *Casino Royale*, he rarely became involved in any of the industry's colossal follies except for Dino De Laurentiis's grandiose scheme to film the entire Bible, which never progressed

beyond the first chapters of Genesis, with Huston narrating and playing Noah in *In the Beginning* (1966).

He had taken up a long abandoned acting career a few years earlier
to play the title role in Otto Preminger's *The Cardinal,* and apparently
he relished the experience for he has played small and large roles in
his own later films, appeared in more than two dozen films for other
directors (most notably in Roman Polanski's *Chinatown*), and narrated
documentaries like *John Huston's Dublin.* Few film luminaries have
had such long, varied, and spectacular careers, so that no explanation
is needed for our joining the American Film Institute in honoring John
Huston's apparently inexhaustible talents.

One justification for this particular study, however, is that—as Scott
Hammen points out—unlike most earlier tributes to a director who is
perhaps even more famous for his free-wheeling lifestyle than for his
solid accomplishments, it leaves the colorful anecdotes about Huston
to their earlier tellers and continues the AFI tribute by focusing on the
enduring quality of John Huston's work as a film director.

                                                                W. F.

Preface

THIS IS NOT a book about the life of John Huston.

A book about the life of John Huston is obliged to begin with a re-telling of his fabulous beginnings—stories of his grandfather's winning a Missouri town in a poker game, of the director-to-be playing Russian roulette with Mexican cavalry officers, winning and losing fortune and glory in the worlds of theater, crapshooting, journalism, and equitation, all before the age of thirty.

There exists not the tiniest parallel between the life of this book's subject and that of its author, but a small coincidence has convinced me to dispense with a recounting of Huston's early adventures. In 1932, according to at least four books about John Huston, he lived in Paris. Fifty years later I am living in the same city and so am particularly curious about this period in my subject's life. According to William F. Nolan, his first biographer, Huston spent a year and a half in the city and "The French period was more 'serious' than he likes to admit. Huston studied oil painting with an abiding passion; he found, in art, a clarity and order wholly lacking in his rootless existence."[1]

Another biography by Stuart Kaminsky, published a decade later, is somewhat less forthcoming on the episode. "Huston made his way to Paris," he reports simply, "where he lived for a year and a half."[2] If Kaminsky is more circumspect than Nolan, Axel Madsen in his biography of 1978, repeats Nolan's account and embellishes: "The French period was more serious than John would like to admit. He studied painting with passion and in art found a clarity and order wholly missing from his own life."[3]

In 1977 came yet another—and by far the best—Huston book, a distillation of Huston's own tape-recorded reminiscences by Gerald Pratley. By now the Paris period is so much "more serious than John would like to admit," he barely admits it at all. His only comment is "I made a quick trip to Paris and then I went back to the States."[4]

Presumably the most reliable account of the period is that of Huston himself in his autobiography (1980). Even the cursory reference in the

Pratley interview has now disappeared. Concluding his remembrance of his time in London (whence he had supposedly embarked for the Continent), Huston states: "But we had enough money to buy tickets home, and that's what we did."[5]

John Huston, in 1932, may or may not have lived in Paris; but his escapades there, along with many others in his adventurous life, are part of a myth irrelevant to his work as a film director; and I have chosen not to embroider on this myth, but to look only at what Huston brought to the screen. If such an effort violates the widely held assumption that John Huston's life is more interesting than his films, then so be it.

SCOTT HAMMEN

Paris

Chronology

1906   John Huston born 5 August, in Nevada, Missouri, son of actor Walter Huston and journalist Rhea Gore. Childhood divided between early years in various cities with his mother and later itinerant theatrical life with his father.

1931   Works on scripts of three Universal productions.

1938   Becomes a contract writer for Warner Brothers and works on several scripts—the most important, *High Sierra*.

1941   On the basis of a rough draft of a script, is offered the job of directing the third version of Dashiell Hammett's *The Maltese Falcon*. Its success establishes him as a director at Warner Brothers.

1942   *In This Our Life*. Before his third Warner film, *Across the Pacific*, is finished, he accepts a commission in the United States Army Signal Corps on active duty. Makes the first of his wartime documentaries, *Report from the Aleutians*.

1943   Sent to Italy to document the entry of the American forces into Rome, he instead produces a horrific account of infantry combat, *The Battle of San Pietro*.

1945   Assigned to produce a film showing that veterans could be cured of psychiatric wounds as well as physical ones, he movingly documents the damage the war has done to men's spirits in *Let There Be Light*. (The War Department suppressed the film until 1981.)

1948   Shoots *The Treasure of the Sierra Madre* on location in Mexico, one of the first Hollywood-produced films to be made outside the United States. Also visits Florida for *Key Largo*.

1949   *We Were Strangers*.

1950   Directs an exemplary film noir, *The Asphalt Jungle*. James Agee in *Life* hails Huston as a major force in American film.

1951   Battles with MGM to bring his version of Stephen Crane's *The Red Badge of Courage* to the screen, then leaves for Africa before postproduction is complete.

1952   Shoots *The African Queen,* his greatest popular success, in Africa.

1953   Experiments with color cinematography in Paris in *Moulin Rouge.* Also plays around in *Beat the Devil.*

1956   Films *Moby Dick* in Ireland, where he establishes residence and eventually becomes a citizen.

1957   *Heaven Knows, Mr. Allison.*

1958   *The Barbarian and the Geisha. The Roots of Heaven.*

1960   *The Unforgiven.* Returns to Hollywood to collaborate with Arthur Miller on *The Misfits,* released in 1961.

1963   Pursues his interest in psychoanalysis, shooting *Freud* in Vienna. *The List of Adrian Messenger.*

1964   *The Night of the Iguana.*

1966   Directs, narrates, and plays the role of Noah in Dino De Laurentiis's first installment of *The Bible, In the Beginning,* a venture that proceeded no further.

1967   *Casino Royale,* a James Bond spoof. Further Technicolor experiments in *Reflections in a Golden Eye,* shot in Italy.

1969   *Sinful Davey. A Walk with Love and Death.*

1970   *The Kremlin Letter.*

1972   Returns to the scene of his boyhood boxing career in southern California to film *Fat City. The Life and Times of Judge Roy Bean.*

1973   *The Mackintosh Man.*

1975   Realizes a decades-long desire to adapt Kipling's *The Man Who Would Be King,* shot in Morocco. *Independence.*

1979   On a tiny budget, with an unknown cast, shoots in Macon, Georgia, one of his best films, adapted from Flannery O'Conner's novel *Wise Blood* (released in 1980).

1980   *Phobia.* Narrates *John Huston's Dublin.*

1981   *Victory.*

1982   *Annie.*

1984   *Under the Volcano.* Starts filming *Prizzi's Choice.*

1

Hollywood Writer

WHEN JOHN HUSTON BEGAN his Hollywood career in earnest in the late 1930s, it was not exactly as a newcomer. He had early aspirations to be a writer. In his autobiography he mentions having had a story published in March 1929 in H. L. Mencken's *American Mercury,* a most prestigious literary journal. John's father, the distinguished actor Walter Huston, purportedly had given his twenty-three-year-old son's story to Ring Lardner, who passed it on to Mencken. But if names like Mencken and Lardner suggest that Huston was a rising literary star, he did not rise far. He professed to regard writing as just a "way of making money," an attitude that obviously kept him open to more lucrative occupations. Journalism, as a short stint on the *New York Graphic* proved, was not, however, among them.

More promising was an offer from Hollywood: producer Herman Shumlin, whom John had met in New York, had, like Walter, just gone West to convert some of his Broadway prestige into movie dollars. Shumlin convinced his new employer, Samuel Goldwyn, to engage Huston as a writer. But before a single word written by John Huston was to grace the script of a Goldwyn picture, relations between the studio head and Shumlin deteriorated. The latter returned to New York and left his protégé unemployed.

Again father attempted to procure employment for son. Under contract to Universal to make a film called *A House Divided* (1931), Walter Huston urged his offspring to improve upon the existing script. The production's director was another Hollywood neophyte, William Wyler, who was willing to take all the help he could get. At the beginning of a long and prestigious career, Wyler welcomed Huston's aid and helped him win a contract from Universal chief Carl Laemmle, Jr. The results were satisfactory and John was assigned work on another script for his father, an adaptation from a crime novel by W. R. Burnett. Huston's talents were later to combine memorably with Burnett's, but *Law and Order* (1932) did not do much for the career of its coscenarist. Nor did two subsequent efforts at Universal, *Murders in the Rue*

The young John Huston already establishing his role as the traveling director. Courtesy of the Museum of Modern Art, Film Stills Archive.

Morgue (1932) and *Laughing Boy,* a project about the Navajo Indians devised by Huston and Wyler, which never reached the screen. Huston's contract with Universal expired; a project with Darryl F. Zanuck to write on the life of P. T. Barnum foundered and there followed an ill-fated stint at Gaumont-British, in London.

"I was twenty-eight years old now, and at loose ends," recalled Huston. After another try at journalism and a crack at acting in a WPA Federal Theater production in Chicago, Huston was brought back to the movies by William Wyler, who was working on *Jezebel* (1938). In this Bette Davis vehicle, the star plays an alluring Southern belle who toys with the affections of Henry Fonda. Displeased with some elements of the script given him, Wyler asked Huston to polish it and, back in Hollywood, Huston suddenly seemed to find his groove. Happy with his work on *Jezebel,* its producer, Henry Blanke, put Huston onto the Warner Brothers payroll as a writer.

The Warners studio, like its rivals, was organized to turn out motion pictures with as much quality as speed and cost efficiency would allow. Its writing department, like its other divisions, was expected to provide not expressions of a single author's personal style, but collaborative efforts that satisfied everyone. However idiosyncratic a personality John Huston was at the time, his quirks had no place on the Warners assembly line. "If I wrote at night," he later bragged a bit, "I would arrive at the studio the following morning around ten or eleven o'clock. This was not the Warners way. They liked to regiment their troops. Writers were supposed to be in at 9:30 in the morning . . ." (*OB,* 72). That the same bombastic storyteller who spun tales of fabulous drinking, gambling, and globetrotting, should content himself with the boast that he dared show up for work at Warners thirty minutes late is inadvertent testimony to the strictness with which the studio kept its employees in line.

After *Jezebel,* Huston was assigned to a story with ties to the gangster genre Warners had pioneered, *The Amazing Dr. Clitterhouse* (1938), then to two projects in another favored Warners area, the dramatized biography. *Juarez* (1938) told the story of a hero of Mexican history; *Dr. Ehrlich's Magic Bullet* (1940) treated the life of the man who had discovered a cure for syphilis and its screenplay received an Oscar nomination. And then came a still more notable project, *Sergeant York* (1941), directed by Howard Hawks and starring Gary Cooper in the title role as America's greatest hero of World War I.

While few rivaled the power of Hawks's work, all the other productions Huston worked on during this period were worthy examples of what an efficient, quality-conscious studio at the height of its prosperity could create. Discussing them as the work of John Huston, however, is a difficult matter. While a director can be assumed to have been physically present during the shooting of a film and thus, even if by default, influencing all facets of the film, no such assumptions can be made about a writer. Screenplay credit could go to the writer of an abandoned first draft, a contributor only to certain scenes or, as in the case of Huston on *Jezebel,* to a writer called in at the last minute to make minor alterations. To apply the term *Hustonian* with any consistency even to the films Huston directed is difficult.

High Sierra (1941)

Yet if a Huston influence on the films he helped write is not detectable, the reverse is not true. There is an unquestionable link between the fifth and last project of his predirectorial career and a number of the films he was to go on to direct. *High Sierra* was in one sense just another installment in the ongoing tradition of Warners gangster pictures, but it was to play a principal role in revitalizing that tradition. And Huston's involvement in the final draft of its script not only acquainted him with the genre, but also brought him into contact with people who were to shape the rest of his career. *High Sierra* was Huston's final step up the ladder to the role of Hollywood director.

The original story and first version of *High Sierra*'s script were by W. R. Burnett, whose story had been the basis for Huston's early Universal effort *Law and Order.* Burnett's impact on the movies had not been made by that film but by a screen version of another of his novels, *Little Caesar* (1930). That saga of the rise of a small-time hoodlum to the status of all-powerful crime lord had established the career of Edward G. Robinson and made stories of fast cars, daring crimes, and ferocious gun battles an enduring staple of screen spectacle. In *Little Caesar* the gangster film attained a level of nihilism and violence that so frightened even its own producers that the industry resolved to devise some form of self-censorship. Their solution, the Production Code, ruled that crime dramas must, even as they excited their viewers, remind them that their subjects were reprehensible. Such moral vigilance dampened some of the genre's spirit in the years after *Little Caesar,* but with *High Sierra* that spirit suddenly revived with a vengeance. Responsible, in addition to Burnett and Huston, were several other equally interesting men.

The film's producer was Mark Hellinger, an ex-journalist who had covered the New York underworld firsthand before putting his familiarity with the milieu at the service of highly realistic crime movies. Its director was Raoul Walsh, whose apprenticeship as a handler of screen action had been served at the beginning of the century at the Biograph Studios with D. W. Griffith and who later played John Wilkes Booth in *The Birth of a Nation* (1915). In watching Walsh at work,

Huston was learning skills of directing narrative film handed down directly from the medium's father.

The Production Code had expressly forbidden the portrayal of the legendary gangster John Dillinger (who had been killed in 1934) on the screen but that did not seem to bother Burnett or Huston; their story borrowed openly from actual incidents in Dillinger's career. Chosen to play the ruthless central figure of the film was George Raft, who, while not the most gifted actor on the Warners payroll, was able to exploit the mystique surrounding his supposedly close connections with the real underworld. Raft, however, refused the role, professing weariness with roles in which he was gunned down by the police (a Production Code requirement for lawbreakers). Raft's refusal opened the door to the making of a screen idol who was to be a key participant in Huston's early career.

Humphrey Bogart at the time was still struggling to break out of the stereotyped villain mold that had been established by the screen version of his stage success *The Petrified Forest* (1936). His menacing leer had thenceforth been a staple element in the best of the Warners gangster pictures, among them *Kid Galahad* (1939), *Angels with Dirty Faces* (1938), *The Roaring Twenties* (1939), and *They Drive by Night* (1940), the latter two of which were directed by Walsh. On the surface, *High Sierra* marked no radical departure for Bogart but, in retrospect, it can be seen as the beginning of his apotheosis as the bad guy with a heart of gold. Since the specter of real-life gangster violence had diminished since the early thirties, *High Sierra* was able to sneak some sympathetic traits into the character of its Dillinger-like subject. And thus Bogart began to develop an image as a tough-as-nails cynic who, at a crucial moment, allows his hidden human decency to shine through. Walsh's film left Bogart and Huston poised on the verge of bigger things and within the year, the first of those things occurred.

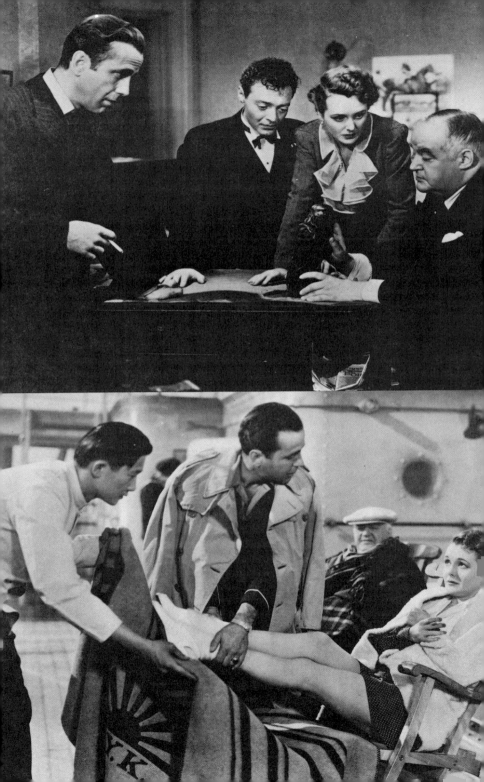

2

Hollywood Director

"There's a girl wants to see you. Her name's Wonderly."
"A customer?"
"I guess so. You'll want to see her anyway: she's a knockout."

THE OPENING LINES of dialogue between a private detective and his secretary that reached moviegoers in early October 1941 had been written well over a decade earlier by a private-eye-turned-writer named Dashiell Hammett. The most striking thing about John Huston's first attempt at directing was how doggedly he stuck to his source. Though officially credited with the film's screenplay, Huston contented himself with an almost literal transcription of Hammett's book. By his own account, in fact, the whole project began when Jack Warner approved an outline of the book, which he mistook for a completed script. Apocryphal or not, the story fits the facts: Huston's *The Maltese Falcon* could hardly have been more loyal to Hammett's.

The Maltese Falcon (1941)

Happy with Huston's work as a screenwriter, Jack Warner had purportedly promised Huston that if he could extract a workable script from the Hammett property, he would be allowed to direct it. The offer was not very risky on Warner's part: the book had already been adapted to the screen twice before (in 1931 under its original title and in 1936 as *Satan Met a Lady*) with neither extraordinary success nor failure. The budget was low, not over $300,000, and the shooting schedule a short six weeks. Huston's task was to stage Hammett's action as briskly and straightforwardly as possible while trusting his cast and crew to keep his inexperience from showing. He knew enough about the rudiments of stagecraft to block out his shots visually and enough about actors to know when to leave them alone. "About half the time," he later recalled, "they would themselves fall into the set-ups that I'd designed and about a quarter of the time I'd have to bring them into those set-ups. The remaining quarter of the time, what they

The Humphrey Bogart–Mary Astor–Sydney Greenstreet trio that made Huston famous: (top) with Peter Lorre in The Maltese Falcon; *(bottom) in Japanese hands in* Across the Pacific. *Courtesy of the Museum of Modern Art, Film Stills Archive.*

7

showed me was better than what I had drawn; something better than
what I had thought out beforehand was forthcoming."[1]

This matter-of-fact approach offers little hint of the exceptional nature of its result: *The Maltese Falcon* was an exemplary mystery thriller
and helped inaugurate a whole genre depicting the dark side of urban
life later to be labeled "film noir." For Huston, it was a directorial
debut, second perhaps only to Orson Welles's *Citizen Kane*, released
the same year, in the praise and expectation it generated.

The comparison with Welles is illuminating for the dissimilarity of
both the two productions and the directing careers each launched. *Citizen Kane* was a tour de force that bent every element of the moviemaking process to its director's ends; Welles imposed his personality
as forcefully behind the camera as he did in the role of Charles Foster
Kane in front of it. He attacked the new medium with a reckless ar-
rogance that could never have been sustained, and he was soon called
to account. By the end of the decade his name, as director, was on only
three more films.

Huston, by contrast, with his self-effacing willingness to listen to his
actors, made his first film conspicuous precisely for the absence of
flourish and bravado. Its impact came from having reduced the medium to one of its most fundamental functions: direct, economical recording of a good story played by equally good performers. If Welles
risked everything in his first venture, Huston risked nothing and, by
the end of the decade, he had almost three times as many films to his
credit as did Welles.

The metaphor one might evoke is that of the grasshopper and the
ant. And, as it happens, it is a central one in an article that appeared
in *Life* magazine in 1950. "Undirectable Director," as the piece was
titled, was the single most influential piece of criticism on Huston's
career. Because its author was James Agee, the most admired of American film critics, and because it is often regarded as having, in fellow
critic Andrew Sarris's words, "canonized Huston prematurely," the
Life article has almost always been cited in appraisals of Huston's career. How peculiar then that it should begin with a fable in which
Huston is totally miscast.

Wrote Agee: "The ant, as every sluggard knows, is a model citizen.
His eye is fixed unwaveringly upon Security and Success, and he gets
where he is going. The grasshopper, as every maiden aunt delights in
pointing out, is his reprehensible opposite number: a hedonistic jazz
baby, tangoing along primrose paths to a disreputable end. . . . Walter
Huston's son John, one of the ranking grasshoppers of the Western
Hemisphere is living proof of what a lot of nonsense that can be. He
has beaten the ants at their own game and then some, and he has
managed that blindfolded, by accident, and largely just for the hell of

it."[2] Agee's characterization did wonders for the Huston myth but he might have been better cast as the ant opposite Welles's grasshopper. The latter's consistent contempt for the industry's rules dramatizes by contrast Huston's measured survivalist approach. Though Huston, with Agee's help, may have cultivated an image of a wild desperado, such an image cannot explain how, over four turbulent decades in the film business, he kept tackling and, in general, acquitting himself honorably with virtually every kind of material a producer ever wanted to bring to the screen. If Huston was an ant, he was not an ignoble one. If he was really a grasshopper, he was a strangely methodical one.

The chief beneficiary of Huston's workmanlike approach to the Dashiell Hammett thriller was Humphrey Bogart. As in his first professional contact with Huston, *High Sierra*, Bogart owed his good fortune to the bad judgment of George Raft. Raft's objection could not have been to getting gunned down by the police, since Hammett's protagonist survives, so it was probable that, as Huston remembered it, he just "didn't want to work under an inexperienced director." But though Raft may have feared Welles-like impetuousness, Bogart surely knew Huston well enough to know his beginner's uncertainty would take a different form. "I had my set-ups," Huston remarked simply, "but I didn't want to be rigid in my approach" (*OB*, 78). Bogart already knew his way around the soundstages and he now had the dual advantage of both working with a director who was willing to give him free rein and being cast in a role that, for almost the first time in his screen career, allowed him to be not just a slightly sympathetic villain but a no-holds-barred hero.

Bogart did not have much physically in common with the Sam Spade described by Hammett as looking "rather pleasantly like a blond satan," but the personality of the author's protagonist could not have been better suited to the actor. For the first of what were to be many times in Huston's films, an actor was to seem so perfectly suited to the character he played that reading the book creates the impression that the author had written with him specifically in mind. And in the case of *The Maltese Falcon*, the resemblance was to extend to virtually everyone in the cast. Peter Lorre, the great veteran of the giant UFA Studios of pre-Nazi Berlin and, in Huston's view, "one of the finest and most subtle actors I have ever worked with," seemed not to be acting at all as the character Hammett described as "a small-boned dark man of medium height. His hair was black and smooth and very glossy. His features were Levantine. . . ." And if only Lorre could have been Hammett's oily Levantine, only Sydney Greenstreet, making his movie debut at sixty-one after forty years on the stage, could have been his Casper Gutman. He was, wrote Hammett, "flabbily fat with bulbous pink cheeks and lips and chin and neck, with a great soft egg of a belly

that was all his torso, and pendant cones for arms and legs. As he advanced to meet Spade all his bulbs rose and fell separately with each
step, in the manner of clustered soap bubbles not yet released from
the pipe through which they had been blown. His eyes, made small
by fat puffs around them, were dark and sleek. . . . His voice was a
throaty purr."

To argue however that Huston had only to sit back and allow a perfectly assembled cast to read Hammett's words in order to make a faultless film is to take the idea of his accidental good fortune too far. There
were surely many mistakes that Huston could have made but did not.
The film, for example, never wastes a second of time or a square foot
of space. Every exchange of words is brisk and every shot is tightly
framed around its subjects; such economy of gesture and movement
could never have resulted from directorial indifference. The Warners
set designers, with their nondescript facsimiles of San Francisco offices
and hotel rooms, had not given Huston much to work with and neither
did his budget or shooting schedule. And if the story had so much
inherent impact that anyone could have succeeded with it, then surely
the two earlier versions would have. It was Huston, one must conclude, who had the instinct about where to place the camera to sustain
dramatic tension and how to move it, sometimes almost imperceptibly,
to intensify his actors' movements. It must also have been Huston who
maintained a breathless pace both in the rhythm of the dialogue and
in the cutting between sequences.

There was undoubtedly an element of happy accident to Huston's
being able to make his directing debut with material to which he was
so clearly temperamentally suited, but he needed more than just his
temperament. What Dashiell Hammett's story of a mysterious black
bird demanded (and did not receive in its earlier screen treatments)
was a director smart enough to realize the original dialogue could not
be improved, humble enough to listen to his actors, visually resourceful enough to stage scenes quickly and effectively, and finally, relaxed
enough not to take the whole thing too seriously and thereby miss out
on the pure fun of such a basically preposterous story. In John Huston,
The Maltese Falcon found all of these.

In This Our Life (1942)

Perhaps because it is so incompatible with the Huston-as-grasshop-
per myth, his next project, *In This Our Life*, has been rarely discussed
by the director's admirers. Those who have written in praise of his
"genius" with *The Maltese Falcon*, an essentially faithful adaptation
from a book by Dashiell Hammett, are mute about his doing exactly
the same thing a few months later with a book by Ellen Glasgow. The

film's reputation further suffers from Huston's own disregard; "I never cared for it," he says cursorily in his autobiography. And still another handicap is the larger lack of esteem for the genre to which it belongs, condescendingly referred to as "the women's picture." Unlike film noir, which *The Maltese Falcon* helped define, the "women's picture" was well established, and Glasgow's novel earned her a Pulitzer Prize just as Huston's film of it reached theaters. No glory could be derived from Huston's having triumphed over a restrictive budget and a less than stellar cast, for the production was given the studio's best treatment. Huston had hit, as he put it, "the big time."

The adaptation from Glasgow's novel was done by Howard Koch, the writer of Orson Welles's notorious radio broadcast of 1938 based on H. G. Wells's *The War of the Worlds*. Koch was later to achieve fame for his work on the script of *Casablanca* (1942). Huston had met him years earlier when he had taken a part in a play written by Koch produced by the WPA Federal Theater project in Chicago. Immediately afterward Huston had gone to Hollywood to work with William Wyler on the Bette Davis vehicle *Jezebel* so there was a certain symmetry to the fact that when Warners, on Huston's recommendation, brought Koch to Hollywood, his first assignment was in the same vein as Huston's first with Wyler. In *Jezebel*, Huston helped Wyler help Davis win an Oscar as a spoiled and willful Southern belle. In *In This Our Life*, Koch helped Huston help Davis play virtually the same role, only this time she was only to earn an Oscar nomination.

The setting was a romanticized version of the old South, a setting with which Warners' (and indeed every big studio's) art department had had ample experience. And from its opening scene, the film is as rich in material accoutrements—houses, clothing, furniture—as *The Maltese Falcon* was impoverished. No expense was spared in the display of Warners' most prized female stars and, whatever his instincts, there was absolutely no way Huston could have given the film the masculine qualities with which his name was to be traditionally associated. Bette Davis commanded every scene in a way that suggests Huston did not so much direct her as stay out of her way. Her only competition came from Olivia de Havilland, playing the "good" sister opposite Davis's evil schemer.

The trade press of the day saw no diminution in Huston's talent, commenting that he "confirms the promise he displayed in his directorial debut" (*Hollywood Reporter*, 9 May 1942) and "That his splendid direction of *The Maltese Falcon* was no flash-in-the-pan becomes a certainty when one sees John Huston's second directorial effort" (*Showman's Trade Review*, 15 May 1942). Once again he had, according to the *New York Herald* (6 June 1942), "followed the novel laboriously in his staging." The difference between Huston's first and second effort, in fact, lay almost entirely in that between their respective sources and very little in his handling of them. The complicated story—involving nonstop tragedies to the "good" sister and continual malevolence from the "bad" one—had nothing to do with what were later to be proposed as Huston's consistent personal themes; but simply having told it clearly and energetically was a testament to a director's skill, especially one working with a big budget and the studio's top stars for the first time.

The one aspect of the film with which Huston professed to take pride was what, for its time, was a progressive view of race relations. "It was the first time, I believe, that a black character was presented as anything other than a good and faithful servant or comic relief," Huston stated. His claim may not be categorically true but the film does give ample attention to the character played by Ernest Anderson, one of the rare black actors to escape from the stereotype defined by Stepin Fetchit. He is a maid's son who harbors the ambition of becoming a lawyer and is encouraged by the "good" character ("That's wonderful," says de Havilland, "I know you'll be a lawyer someday, Perry") and used as point of reference to define the "bad" ones ("You've got everything that boy wants and you sit here feeling sorry for yourself," Davis is told). His mother, played by Hattie McDaniel, is given a scene in which she makes a reasonable plea to the totally unreasonable Davis and is, of course, rebuffed. In another sequence the spoiled white girl is eloquently reprimanded by the black lawyer-to-be. These two scenes were not to remain in every print of the film.

Released in a climate of more than normally uneasy race relations (there had been clashes between white and black draftees at several army bases during the mobilization for war), the film caused uneasiness among Warners executives. Curiously, they allowed it to be released uncut to white audiences but decided to excise the two above-named sequences from the prints of the film shown in black neighborhoods of New York. The rationale apparently was that, while black audiences were quite used to seeing insulting images of themselves on the screen, the sight of articulate blacks might cause trouble. Harlem newspapers vainly raised their voices in protest.

For all its "woman's picture" melodrama, *In This Our Life* bears some noble traces of the Warners action film tradition that Huston had learned about from its grand master, Raoul Walsh. The wildness of the natural world as a metaphor for the characters' inner turmoil, a key element in Walsh's *High Sierra*, is deftly handled by Huston as de Havilland and George Brent cling desperately to each other while perched high in the Blue Ridge Mountains and watch a distant forest fire burn out of control below them. The film's climactic sequence, a high-speed car chase between the crazed Davis and the police, also bears the flair of the more "masculine" tradition of action filmmaking.

Huston, in short, may not have been working within his preferred arena, but made the best of the opportunities at hand. The production is sturdily constructed, well paced, tightly edited, and lushly scored.

Across the Pacific (1943)

The director's next project, *Across the Pacific*, unlike its predecessor, added fuel to the Huston mystique and is an undisguised reprise of his first film. There had been talk, mainly on the part of the Warners publicity department, of the imminent production of *The Further Adventures of the Maltese Falcon*, which would reassemble the original's cast and director. It never came to pass under that title but was, in effect, done just the same in the form of an adaptation of a serial that had run for a while in the *Saturday Evening Post*. The film cannot strictly be considered a sequel, for it has little in common with the world of Dashiell Hammett. But its characters are almost unchanged with only the absence of Peter Lorre marring the reunion of Bogart as the savvy hero, Mary Astor as a lady whose whispered endearments may be treacherous, and Sydney Greenstreet as an obese aesthete whose impeccable manners mask a ruthless will. Times had changed: movies in general had become more interested in cheering on the nation's war effort than shedding light on the evils of its urban underworld. And Hammett's essentially bitter and serious tone was supplanted by a parodistic and flippant one. The Huston wit, earlier held in check in deference to Hammett, had free rein when working from a source as lowly as a magazine serial.

That wit begins as soon as the film's title has flashed onto the screen: the phrase *Across the Pacific* has not the slightest relation to the story that follows. The original tale had indeed traversed the Pacific Ocean to conclude in Hawaii, but the events of 7 December 1941 had ruled out a story about thwarting a Japanese plot to destroy Pearl Harbor. So the ship bearing the drama's participants was obliged to sail no further than Panama (Bogart was said to have quipped "Let's hurry up and get this thing over with before the Canal goes too"). *Across the Pacific* takes place along the Atlantic.

Though tentative at first about touching on political affairs, Hollywood by 1941 had begun to raise its voice against fascism. Knowing the enemy, however, was not the same as knowing the future. Any sudden turn of events might render a script ridiculous or in questionable taste. The only solution was to rewrite stories to keep them current until the very moment they went before the cameras and then simply hope that the real world did not betray them too much from that point on. Such was the burden of Richard Macauley, the Warners writer charged with the adaptation of the *Saturday Evening Post* serial about Japanese sabotage. The film's opening takes great pains to fix the story's date: according to an extremely obvious calendar, it is 17 November 1941. The action that follows takes place over the next two and a half weeks, coming to a climax on 6 December. As a final irony, a newspaper of that date is shown with headlines announcing the progress of peace talks with Japan. In at least this one instance, the studio's product managed to stay in step with the national mood.

That mood, in the late summer of 1942, was one of continued outrage against the aggressions of the Japanese and *Across the Pacific* railed against them obstreperously. Surely its recriminations answered a deep-seated need in its audiences, for the news from the front was not good. Yet from the perspective of forty years, the film's characterization of anyone oriental as treacherous and evil seems to go beyond wholesome flag waving. An innocent-looking travel agency decorated with picturesque posters urging tourists to visit Japan turns out to be a nest of vicious spies. Sydney Greenstreet's unctuous enthusiasm for a precious black bird in the earlier film is now turned toward Asian culture. The Japanese, he pedantically observes, "make great servants" and are a "wonderful little people, greatly misunderstood." Later in the story Bogart confirms the notion that "they all look alike" and Mary Astor speculates without sounding at all convinced that maybe "they *do* have emotions—just like us." Wartime frenzy may explain the crudeness of these remarks but it's hard to imagine the Germans, with whom Americans were just as much at war, being described as making great servants or being a "wonderful little people."

The most disturbing characterization, however, in light of what was later to be revealed about American policy, was that of the Nisei, Americans born to parents of Japanese ancestry. They are embodied in the film by Joe, a character more dangerous and duplicitous than the actual Japanese from whom he is distinguishable only by his totally American English. He is, on the surface, amiable and ingratiating, full of boyish energy and good humor, but below the surface lurks a monster. In a not-very-subtle metaphor for the beast within, Joe wears a pair of very thick glasses that, when shot in close-up as he adjusts them on his nose, magnify his features grotesquely. (The same trick, minus the racial overtones, was used at about the same time by Orson Welles to add menace to his villain in *Journey into Fear*, 1943.) Joe's speech, that of any bright and gregarious college boy and full of jokes and colloquialisms, seems to indicate that the oriental threat has fully penetrated American society and the viewer can only feel thankful that Joe's physiognomy betrays his demonic nature.

In the film's context, the equation of Asian features with treason even on the part of native-born Americans is, like so much else in the movie, comic. What is less funny is the fact that, at about the time of the film's release, the then attorney general of California, Earl Warren, issued an order requiring the rounding up of all Americans of Japanese descent for internment in concentration camps. While they did not suffer the fate of Jews in Germany, their lives were destroyed in subtler ways—their property confiscated, their livelihood taken away, their families broken up, and their freedom as American citizens denied. Subsequent revelations about California's solution to its "Nisei problem" take much of the fun out of watching *Across the Pacific*'s Joe doublecross his American friends. A final irony was that the very internment policy the film was doing so much to endorse threatened to disrupt its production. Authorities sought to detain the Nisei on the Warners payroll and only the studio's vociferous protests gave them a temporary reprieve in order to go on playing Japanese spies. As soon as shooting was completed though, they were hauled off to the camps.

Yet if the anti-Japanese bombast can be overlooked, Huston's third film has some agreeable qualities. In a felicitious way, *Across the Pacific* combines the pleasures of suspenseful intrigue not unlike *The Maltese Falcon* with a comic playfulness that seems to mock it. Those elements that establish the suspense—the turbulent preparations for a huge freighter's setting out to sea at midnight, the fetid atmosphere of a run-down hotel in the Canal Zone, a smoky movie house where the noisy violence on the screen masks quieter but much deadlier acts in the dark rows in front of it (a juxtaposition Alfred Hitchcock used to similarly effective ends in his *Saboteur* the same year)—are handled deftly. But just as much attention is paid to the material's parodistic, comic-strip possibilities. *The Maltese Falcon* had had its share of humor (one thinks of Spade's response when he is asked to speculate about who committed a murder: "My guess might be excellent or it might be crummy, but Mrs. Spade didn't raise any children dippy enough to make guesses in front of a district attorney, an assistant district attorney, and a stenographer"), but its humor was realistic—that of a streetwise detective. The banter between Bogart and Mary Astor in their second outing together has a more epigrammatic tone, a little too clever for a workaday private eye. "Are you getting sick?" Bogart inquires of Astor who has not yet got her sea legs for the ocean voyage. "How do girls usually act when you kiss them?" she responds. And while most action movies kept the gun-as-phallus references low-key, Bogart and Greenstreet are not at all reticent. Clutching his weapon at the level of his crotch, the effeminate Greenstreet points out: "Even *I* have a gun!" Brandishing his in the same position, Bogart points out: "Mine's bigger than yours." The censors could only have let such remarks pass because they looked far more innocuous on the printed page than when spoken by two masters of the double entendre under the waggish direction of another.

Across the Pacific is not the only witty and expertly constructed Hollywood movie to have passed into relative oblivion, but considering the extraordinary renown of a very similar production, the lack of attention seems more undeserved. Casablanca (1942), one of the world's best-loved and most-watched movies, rolled off the Warners assembly line right behind Huston's film. Its producer, Hal B. Wallis, was the man who backed Huston's first scriptwriting efforts at the studio and then produced his first two films. Its scenarist, Howard Koch, had come to Hollywood at Huston's invitation and written his second film. Its star, Humphrey Bogart, owed his stardom to Huston, and the character that made him legendary in Casablanca was essentially unchanged from the one he had played for Huston just a few months earlier.

Huston had presented Bogart at first as an alienated American, devoid of ideals; Casablanca does the same. Both characters are named Rick and both wear what appears to be the same trenchcoat. In Across the Pacific Bogart is gradually revealed to be not an unscrupulous opportunist but a brave man ready to risk all for his beliefs—precisely the transformation that occurs in Casablanca. A crucial difference, it must be admitted, is the nature of the love interest in the two tales. It is hard, for example, to imagine the dewy-eyed Ingrid Bergman of the later film taking delight in her Rick being sick from overdrinking and exclaiming, as Mary Astor does, "This is the happiest moment of my life. Is there anything I can do to make you sicker?" One thing Across the Pacific is not, even when it pretends to be, is sentimental and it is to that quality that Casablanca owes its immortality.

The story of the production's ending is one of those that have become a centerpiece of Huston folklore. As the tale goes, shooting had almost been completed when Huston, who had already enlisted in the army, received orders to report immediately to Washington. As a joke on whoever Warners assigned to complete the film (it turned out to be Vincent Sherman), Huston decided to make Bogart's plight totally hopeless. Huston guessed correctly that the studio would be unwilling to go to the expense of a lot of reshooting to make his escape from his Japanese captors plausible, so Sherman had to invent something outlandish to allow for a happy ending. "From that point on," Huston loved to point out, "the picture lacked credibility." What mars the neatness of the joke, however, is the fact that very little of the material was strong on credibility to begin with and so a few slightly more preposterous heroics do not stand out.

3

At War

BY APRIL 1942, Huston no longer belonged to a world where eccentric behavior and tempestuous love affairs provided welcome grist for the publicity mill. At the Washington headquarters of the United States Army Signal Corps he was instead enmeshed in a faceless machine that was to offer him little middle ground between dying figuratively of boredom and dying literally in combat. For the first few months, Huston did the former as he impatiently anticipated an assignment. If the government in general was poorly organized for such a rapid mobilization for war, the particular branch in which Huston found himself was even more unprepared than most.

While Hollywood in the late thirties had been providing the most sophisticated entertainment in the world, the German propaganda ministry in Berlin had been using motion pictures quite differently. German audiences, and later those in the countries Hitler's armies invaded, were viewing works of propaganda that relentlessly drove home a message of total Nazi invulnerability. Though both the British and American governments had long been involved in documentary filmmaking, neither, when war was declared against Germany, was prepared to argue its case in movie theaters as effectively as the enemy. When the necessity for such an effort became clear, it was in some ways too late: there were simply not enough combat cameramen in the field to produce timely footage. President Roosevelt knew an extraordinary effort was called for, so, instead of merely bolstering the resources of those in charge of the existing military film unit, the army Signal Corps, he bypassed them entirely and went straight to the moviemaking center of the world—Hollywood. Those best able to sway peoples' hearts and minds with fictional stories, should, the president reasoned, be equally effective with factual material. Put in charge of the massive task of quickly explaining to over eight million men why they were suddenly in uniform was Frank Capra.

Capra had already proved himself a genius at rousing popular feeling for the simple virtues of American democracy in a series of tales focus-

Huston foreshadows Italian neorealism in two scenes from
his wartime documentary The Battle of San Pietro.
Courtesy of the Museum of Modern Art, Film Stills Archive.

19

ing on honest, upright men pitted against powerful, cynical foes. In
Mr. Deeds Goes to Town (1936), *Mr. Smith Goes to Washington* (1940),
and *Meet John Doe* (1941), Capra had turned Gary Cooper and Jimmy
Stewart into icons for an idealistic and courageous America ready to
take on any foe. It was exactly the message newly inducted soldiers
needed to hear and the films coordinated by Capra that formed the
"Why We Fight" series (1942–45) proved that the line between Hollywood artifice and official documentary was very easy to cross.

Huston's first assignment with the Capra unit, however, when after
months of frustrating delay it finally came, could not have been farther
from the studio soundstages in either miles, climate, or spirit. He was
instructed to leave for the Aleutian Islands, the long archipelago jut-
ting out southwesterly from the coast of Alaska. The barren, frigid little
dots of land were not of great strategic importance, but they were the
American territory nearest to that of the enemy. Two of the islands
farthest out on the chain, in fact, were already in Japanese hands and
serving as an airbase for forays over the North Pacific. To retaliate, an
American base had been established on the inhospitable island of Adak
from which bombing raids were to be launched. Huston's mission was
to record the life among those who maintained the base and those who
used it to begin perilous fights in what Huston described as "the storm-
pot of the Western world."

Report from the Aleutians (1943)

When the director and his crew first arrived on Adak, the Japanese
did not know the American base existed. But in the first instance of a
kind of stormy petrel syndrome that was to characterize Huston's
whole army experience, the base was discovered by a Japanese recon-
aissance plane soon after his arrival and from that moment on, aerial
attack was a constant possibility. But the enemy was no more dangerous than the weather. In the days before radar was perfected, pilots
maneuvered with only compasses to guide them. The losses of aircraft
just trying to reach Adak were high: Huston reported that out of one
group of twelve B-26 bombers that had set out for Alaska, only three
reached his base and all of them were forced to make crash landings
on the makeshift airstrip. His subject matter appeared to consist of
aborted missions, mechanical breakdowns, enemy gunfire, and
downed planes. Amid the misfortunes, Huston tried manning one of
the cameras himself and found that he was particularly maladroit.
"Nothing I ever shot personally as a photographer turned out well,"
he reported (*OB*, 89). Between the brutality of the conditions and his
own total inexperience at documentary filmmaking, nothing augured
well for Huston's first contribution to the war effort.

But *Report from the Aleutians* (1943) was to prove the beginning of a trilogy of Huston war documentaries, which, taken as a whole, form the definitive film on World War II as seen through the eyes of the common soldier. Viewed out of the context of its successors, his first documentary seems to fall into the groove of other army efforts: cheerful, upbeat evidence that its forces were gallantly serving their country. Much evidence is placed on the domestic "melting pot" nature of the operation—"Downeastern accents meet with Southern twangs," as Huston's narration puts it. And the drudgery and boredom of life at the isolated outpost is duly recorded. "Biscuits, barrels full of biscuits," intones Walter Huston's voice on the soundtrack, "no girls, nothing to drink." The men read letters from home, shave in cold water, play the harmonica, while the narration reminds the viewer that the island is no legendary battlefield but, in fact, "next to worthless, except as a pin on a map." The emphasis on routine and unheroic tasks had a kind of lulling quality, but the effect could not have been more deliberate: it is the lull before the storm.

The use of Kodachrome, a glossy, high-contrast color film stock, also serves at first to distract from the deadly reason for assembling the amiable group of men on the desolate island. The sheen of the color images gives a picturesque travelogue quality to the setting. In one shot, planes are even shown landing beneath a spectacular rainbow. And because Kodachrome is a relatively slow film, requiring quite bright light for proper exposure, many of the scenes seem to have been shot on uncharacteristically sunny days, further distancing the viewer from any sense of menace. The choice of film stock may not have been Huston's (none of his Hollywood work up to then had been in color nor were his next two war documentaries) but it has a certain appropriateness nonetheless. Like the rainbow it so vividly records, Kodachrome gives an ebullient mood to the process of going to war that matched that of many of the draftees pictured; they were just boys who had suddenly been offered a chance to travel to exotic corners of the world with all expenses paid. Huston, too, always a great lover of adventure, seemed to have embraced military service as a welcome respite from the artifice of Hollywood and looked first on his assignment as something of a lark. The color, the images of soldiers singing around a campfire, the almost boastful tone of the narration, are in themselves unexceptional. But they serve a very specific dramatic purpose: precisely because the daily life of the common soldier has been so well established, the latter portions of *Report from the Aleutians* and virtually every frame of its sequel, *The Battle of San Pietro* (1944), are doubly unnerving.

The first hint of the disturbing things to come occurs when an ambulance is seen racing up to a disabled plane that has just made a

precarious landing. The effect of the scene is at first disorienting after
the talk about biscuits and letters from home. Even more so is the
subsequent scene: a crude wooden casket being lowered into the
ground. The focus then shifts definitively from the routine nature of
life on the ground to the less benign character of life in the air. Walter
Huston's voice changes tone a bit as he reads his son's words over shots
of bombers readying for take-off: "the stage is set, the curtain going
up, but it is not make-believe. They will be playing for keeps." Pro-
pellers roar into action, nervous hands are shown on the instruments
in one of the bomber's cockpits, and the camera's point of view becomes that of the pilot. "The thunder of engines makes the earth trem-
ble and the ravens rise . . . soon the earth below will blaze with
hatred." There follow extraordinary shots of bombs falling over islands
far below.

The actual bombing missions over Japanese-held Kiska Island form
the climax of *Report from the Aleutians*. To film them, Huston and his
cameraman, Ray Scott, flew more than fifteen missions over enemy
targets. Scott was awarded a decoration for his nine missions in six
days—a schedule more brutal than that of many of the fliers he was
filming. A gunner three feet from where Huston was shooting was
killed by an antiaircraft shell and at least once his plane was forced to
crash land.

The aerial shots of enemy positions under bombardment, the tracer
bullets fired from the bomber's machine guns, smoke billowing from
explosions on the ground, the entire latter part of the film has the
immediacy of the most graphic combat footage in other war documentaries. But unlike many of them, Huston's work is never impersonal,
never celebrates the war as spectacle (by far the easiest thing to do
with aerial footage, which is by its very nature abstract). He continues
to isolate the vulnerable individuals concentrating on the details of
their assigned duties, capturing the way a navigator's hands plot a crucial course across a miniscule map, the way the fingers of a bombardier
clutch at his trigger switch, the way a pilot's eyes nervously scan the
horizon for signs of enemy air pursuit. And it was that very attention
to detail that would give rise to the first of what were to be a long
series of disputes between Huston and his army superiors about his
work.

Although *Report from the Aleutians* provides the requisite optimistic ending, with strains of "Rolling Home" (the song sung around the
campfire) accompanying the announcement that all of the planes that
participated in the mission portrayed returned home safely, there were
still objections. Army authorities could see no reason for Huston having dwelled so long at first on such prosaic activities as latrine digging
and bored cigarette smoking—sequences that had nothing to do with

the grandeur of air supremacy and were, therefore, irrelevant to the film's official intent. But Huston fought stubbornly for the retention of those scenes and, in contrast to his subsequent disagreements with his military superiors, he prevailed. His fight to preserve his images of the banal side of army life suggests that on some level, conscious or not, he knew that those sequences would establish the humanity of the men soon to become just statistics in the grotesque accounting of wartime wins and losses. The loss column may not have been long in the Aleutian campaign, but Huston's war trilogy had just begun.

Tunisian Victory (1943)

Captain Huston returned to Los Angeles to edit, score, and have his father record the narration of his first documentary. The dramatic artifice he had mastered in Hollywood stood him in good stead in strengthening the work's impact and it did no damage to its veracity. The same, however, could not be said for his next assignment, which patently demanded falsification. *Tunisian Victory* was the result of an attempt to cover up the absence of just the kind of footage *Report from the Aleutians* had in abundance. President Roosevelt had reportedly asked to see personally the Signal Corp's coverage of the invasion of North Africa and rather than tell him the truth—that the ship carrying the only footage they had had been sunk—the authorities ordered Capra's unit to come up with a facsimile by staging maneuvers in the Mojave Desert. Huston was instructed to assist Capra in shooting troops pretending to be dodging artillery fire. After staging some aerial warfare at an air base in Florida, Huston took the material, "this trash" as he referred to it, to England where it was to represent the American contribution to a coproduction with the British called *Tunisian Victory*. There was a peculiar irony to this frustrating episode of faked battle in that it was to directly precede Huston's most terrifying encounter with the real thing.

The Battle of San Pietro (1944)

Late in 1943 another assignment reached Huston in London. The successful Allied invasion of North Africa a year before had been followed by the invasion of Sicily and, from there, the Italian mainland. Giddy with success, the Allied command expected to sweep dramatically up the peninsula and they ordered Huston to, in his words, "document the triumphal entry of the American forces into Rome" (*OB*, 107). The campaign had progressed on schedule as far north as Naples, the city to which Huston was first dispatched, but in the mountains along the road to Rome, a vicious surprise lay in store for the Allied

command. The treacherous terrain had been the stage for military confrontations for thousands of years; the means of defending passes and
controlling roads had been studied and perfected by Greek tacticians
as early as the fifth century B.C. Even though vastly outnumbered, the
Germans had carefully calculated the ways in which they could still
stall the Allied advance and inflict devastating losses. Later military
analysts were to conclude that the whole episode was a tragic waste—
the terrain could simply have been bypassed in the advance against
Germany. But the Allies were emboldened by their early successes and
convinced that by engaging the enemy in southern Italy, they were
drawing him away from more crucial theaters such as the Russian front
and the Atlantic coast of France. Their reasoning proved very costly.

Huston may have bristled at the stupidity of staging fake desert warfare in California, but he was to see stupidity of a far more horrible
sort when assigned to document the Italian "victory." From Naples
Huston set out with his film crew for the front lines about sixty miles
northward on the road to Rome. In a commanding position over the
entrance to the Liri Valley perched the village of San Pietro; the story
of the efforts of American troops to capture that single tiny village was
the subject of Huston's next film. *The Battle of San Pietro* is the most
harrowing account of the infantryman's experience ever put on film. If
its subject was one insignificant village in Italy, its theme was timeless
and universal: the utter futility of war. Its premise was simple: to show
what happens when a direct frontal assault is ordered on an enemy
position that is virtually impregnable to frontal assault. The carnage
that followed was among the worst of the entire war and Huston and
his crew witnessed it and, somehow, survived it.

The film's narration was again written by Huston, but this time he
read it himself. And the quality of his voice is as perfectly suited to the
grim mood of the work as his father's was to the lighter tone of *Report
from the Aleutians*. There is bitter irony in some of the first words that
accompany establishing shots of the village after it has been bombed
into rubble in a futile attempt to dislodge German gun emplacements.
As the camera pans across the shattered remnants of the village's
church, Huston assumes the pedantic air of a tour guide: "Point of
interest—St. Peter's, 1438," he observes, "Note interesting treatment
of the chancel." The "treatment" has been provided not by a Renaissance architect but by a bombardier. Soon though the tone becomes
simply matter-of-fact: "Flood-swollen rivers twisted across the line of
march so that each river seemed like five, with the enemy always looking down our throats. They'd had time to fortify . . . it was up to the
foot soldier." As directly in the line of fire as any of the combatants,

Huston's cameras, shaking from the tremors of exploding shells (and perhaps, too, from the terror of the men operating them), recorded suicidal attempts by individual men to advance up the hill below San Pietro. As the figure of one soldier is lost from view in the smoke of a mortar attack, the camera pans rightward just in time to see another fall to the ground riddled with machine-gun fire. "Volunteer patrols made desperate attempts to reach enemy positions and reduce strongpoints," Huston reports flatly, "Not a single member of any such patrol ever came back alive."

Day after day, Huston scrambled around within range of hostile fire explaining to each of his cameramen what kinds of shots he was looking for. At night, as shells continued to explode outside his tent, he developed and revised his narration. He was, in a sense, working blindly for his exposed footage was sent directly to Washington for processing and he was not to know until he was thousands of miles from the scene whether what he had shot had captured the feeling of the events.

But the quality of his footage was surely a secondary consideration at the time to the more fundamental one of simply staying alive. Death in all its forms became the central subject of *The Battle of San Pietro*. After a group of tanks that had been ordered up a road controlled by German gunners had been destroyed, Huston and crew moved in to view the remains and he later recalled that "there was a boot here— with the foot and part of a leg still in it—a burned torso there, and other parts of what had been human bodies scattered about" (*OB*, 110). Huston recorded the carnage. Before the battle had begun, he had interviewed many of those about to fight it. Later he juxtaposed their voices musing about their hopes for the future with shots of their corpses after the battle. The film crew did not have to search very hard for the dead: the combat unit they followed, the 143d Regiment of the 36th Texas Infantry, required over 1100 replacements for the losses it incurred trying to move up the Liri Valley. Not surprisingly, Huston's unflinching record of the blood bath was also to incur heavy losses.

Safely back in Hollywood, Huston edited his film and then presented it to his military superiors. They were aghast. In condemning *San Pietro*, those who had commissioned it used the most damning insult they could think of: they called it "antiwar." The entire project was on the point of being scuttled when the general of the army, George C. Marshall, requested to see it. Marshall's reaction differed from that of his underlings: "This picture should be seen by every American soldier in training," he declared. "It will not discourage but rather prepare them for the initial shock of combat" (*OB*, 119). The general's reasoning may have been flawed but it saved the film, or at least the better part of it. With Huston's approval, some of the more gruesome sequences were removed, as was the juxtaposition of the men's voices recorded one day with their corpses photographed the next. Less agreeable to the director was the addition of a Dimitri Tiomkin score which included singing by the Mormon Tabernacle Choir and a spoken introduction by General Mark Clark.

Clark's prologue gamely attempted to put the horrors that follow it into a positive light by asserting that the suicidal frontal attacks on San Pietro "succeeded in holding the enemy away from invasion areas" and that, in the end, "the cost was not excessive." The former claim is dubious in light of how few Germans had actually been engaged and the latter raises the frightening question of just what cost Clark would have considered excessive. But neither statement is as peculiar as his concluding one that the Liri Valley bloodbath represented "an inspiring page in our military history."

Looking at *San Pietro*, even in the truncated form in which it was eventually released, calls into question just what kind of inspiration General Clark had in mind. At the film's end, as images of the devastated village fill the screen, Huston's words enforce the sense of desolation. Where other war documentaries carefully balanced their portrayal of war's horrors with reminders of how useful the sacrifices made were in the larger scheme of things (John Ford's *The Battle of Midway* [1942], for example, describes its subject as nothing less than the "Grandest Naval Victory of the World to Date"), Huston glumly points out that after San Pietro was taken there still lay before its decimated attackers "more valleys, more rivers, more towns, a thousand more, and many of those you see here alive will die." His final images though do not show the soldiers who have moved on to die at the foot of the next hill, but observe San Pietro's inhabitants descend from the caves in which they had taken refuge to reclaim what is left of their town. Their home has been left heavily booby-trapped by the retreating Germans and Huston shows one result: wailing villagers pulling a body from the rubble of a building. Another woman is glimpsed walking down a narrow street with a coffin balanced on her head.

Huston's closing words say one thing but seem to mean another: "Children are able to forget quickly," he tells the viewer over shots of the village children. And of the people who must rebuild while living with the threat of unexploded mines, he explains, "it was to free them and their farmlands that we came." But it is never explained what interest the little village would have had for the occupying Germans if there had been no invading Americans. The sudden meaninglessness of a prize long sought after, a theme treated almost whimsically in *The Maltese Falcon*, had received a more sinister treatment. And though

Huston would return to it many times in fictional form, the fact that there was nothing fictional about the village of San Pietro, that the lives lost there were real ones, puts the film on a different plane. And nothing the War Department did before or since dared repeat its terrible message.

Let There Be Light (filmed 1946, released 1981)

The problems of massive demobilization were no simpler than those of mobilization had been four years earlier. But the government now knew that the movie screen could be an effective tool in changing people's attitudes. What they needed however, as thousands of men were being returned to civilian life, was not another "Why We Fight" episode but a kind of "What Happened to Us When We Fought" document to help integrate former soldiers into a peacetime society. One problem in particular was the reluctance of prospective employers to accept men whose war wounds were not just physical. That combat could have produced psychic injuries was largely unacknowledged so, the army felt, a film should be made to point out the efficacy of their psychiatric care. This delicate task fell to the newly promoted Major John Huston.

If the closing sequences of *San Pietro* offered a glimpse of what happened after the American soldiers moved on, the final chapter of Huston's war trilogy catches up with them or at least those of them who survived. Huston addressed a question directly raised by his images of the carnage in the Liri Valley: what effect did it have on those who did not die? The men seen piling bags filled with their dead comrades into the back of a truck seemed emotionless; only the Italian peasants were shown expressing their grief. The unanswered question was how long their emotions could be kept locked inside. *Let There Be Light*, the culmination of Huston's career as a documenter of World War II, tries to find some answers.

"The guns are quiet now. The papers of peace have been signed." The magisterial voice is again that of Walter Huston reading commentary written by his son. On the screen are men, some of them severely disabled, hobbling down the gangplank of a ship. They are, in the narration's words, "the final result of all that fire and metal can do to mortal flesh." The physical wounds are visible and even have a heroic connotation—a "red badge of courage" in the words of Stephen Crane. But there were other casualties limping off the troop transport, "casualties of the spirit," Huston calls them. "Every man has his breaking point," his narration explains, "and these, in their fulfillment of their duties as soldiers, were forced beyond the limits of human endurance."

It was a side of warfare never before acknowledged by official War Department films.

Huston visited a number of veterans' hospitals with psychiatric wards and settled on Mason General Hospital in Brentwood, Long Island, as the setting for a study of how doctors were trying to help "the casualties of the spirit." He was to spend three months there and shoot many hours of film. Cameras, concealed in the hospital's wards, recorded patients' individual encounters with staff psychiatrists as well as group therapy sessions. It was soon apparent that though, as the narration says, "they do not wear the badges of their pain, the crutches, the bandages, the splints, they too are wounded." The patients suffer from a variety of neuroses, some of them created by, others only exacerbated by combat. Though they are veterans of many different battles in many different theaters of war, their testimony again and again seems to recall specific images from *San Pietro*.

"I lost my last buddy up there," recalls one patient urged by his doctor to remember what traumatized him. "They were shelling us. He was the second scout. I was the first scout and I should have been in front of him. . . . After he got killed, I was all right when I was moving forward, but when I stopped, I thought about him lying back there. I don't care if I live." Another subject, under hypnosis, reconstructs the scene that preceded his attack of amnesia. "We were forced to take cover, five of us. One of the boys got hurt." Suddenly the man's face flinches as if in great pain, then he continues, "An explosion, they're carrying me across the field, they're putting me on a stretcher. . . ." Then, in one of the film's most extraordinary sequences, there is shown a young man who has lost the capacity for intelligible speech. With intense prompting by the psychiatrist, he searches for the origin of his problem and finally isolates it: the sound of the letter S, the sound of an explosive shell approaching, the sound of death in combat. Slowly and methodically, the doctor keeps probing, questioning, and encouraging his patient. And then suddenly comes a breakthrough: "I can talk, I can talk! Oh God, listen, I can talk!"

The recording of the encounters between patients and doctors is so direct and charged with emotion that *Let There Be Light* becomes a film unlike any other. Because it goes inside its subjects, ferreting out things before a movie camera that people generally keep hidden, the film departs drastically from the world of the traditional documentary. Such intimate contact with people seems more properly the domain of concocted melodrama where professional actors pretend to give viewers a peak at their private lives. But there is not the slightest element of Hollywood contrivance to the soldiers' words. Their stories are totally credible, particularly when seen as an aftermath to the combat sequences of *San Pietro*. The men in *Let There Be Light* could perhaps

have feigned their mental agony and nervous exhaustion if every one
of them were a Marlon Brando or a James Dean; but Mason General
Hospital was no Actors Studio. What Huston achieved in his last work
of nonfiction filmmaking was a sort of genre unto itself that combined
the impact of the most intense acting with the force of veracity. It was
a fitting climax to his extraordinary work during the war. The army,
however, did not see it that way. Huston went as far as he credibly
could to give the work a happy ending, showing his subjects at the
film's end once again capable of "the healthy old sound of bellyaching."
He had thus come full circle in his trilogy: from the carefree draftees
in the Aleutians with their "biscuits, barrels full of biscuits," through
the worst terror and trauma of battle in Italy, back to good-humored
complaints about "spinach, spinach again" in the mess hall of a hospital
on Long Island. But for the military authorities, the rehabilitation
Huston implied was unacceptable because, though they never admitted as much, the horror of what they needed rehabilitation from was
all too clearly conveyed. Despite the optimistic ending of *Let There Be
Light*, the sense that the war had irremediably scarred men's souls
remains. The message was unwelcome at the Pentagon and, unlike its
predecessor, the film found no highly placed champion like General
Marshall to overrule the consensus that it should be suppressed.

The War Department issued three reasons for withholding release:
that the men who had appeared would bring suit against the government if scenes of their treatment were ever publicly exhibited, that
there would be adverse reaction from the families of those for whom
the psychiatric care had not been successful, and finally and most
frankly, that Huston had, in their words, "pulled a fast one"—in other
words had made yet another film that committed the sin of being "antiwar." Of the three charges, only the last one has much substance. The
men who had been filmed had all signed releases granting their per-
mission and, by all accounts, had been both intrigued and enthusiastic
about the film crew's presence. The ward, in fact, in which Huston had
worked showed a better recovery rate than any other in the hospital,
suggesting the production may have actually had a therapeutic effect.
The second official objection, that some might protest the upbeat conclusion, is even more peculiar since it must have gone against all of
Huston's instincts to imply that every complicated psychiatric disorder
he observed had a simple cure. Had the army allowed it, he almost
certainly would have preferred not to sweeten the ending (a procedure
he avoided whenever possible in his fiction films) and let the viewer
keep worrying about what the war had done to its participants.

Finally the notion that Huston had "pulled a fast one" is interesting
in that it implies that it was his fault for addressing such a disturbing
subject. The mistake, the War Department surely realized, lay not in

what Huston had done, but in allowing him to tackle the subject in the first place. Yet however flimsy and contradictory its reasons, the government stuck by its refusal for thirty-five years. Wrote a frustrated James Agee in 1946, "I don't know what is necessary to reverse this disgraceful decision, but if dynamite is required, then dynamite is indicated."[1] Finally, in 1981, time and the accompanying changes in the ranks of the bureaucracy apparently accomplished what "dynamite" could not. With the belated release of its climactic finale, John Huston's trilogy of men at war could at last be seen integrally for the masterpiece that it is.

4

Rolling Home

THE EFFECTS OF his experiences in World War II were to reverberate through many of Huston's postwar films. He was to study the effects of war on men's psyches in *Key Largo* (1948) and *The Red Badge of Courage* (1951), and further explore the world of psychoanalysis in *Freud* (1963); but there was a more immediate response when he found himself back in the entertainment industry. The army years, he told an interviewer, "gave me a sense of the reality of human behavior as against the conventions that the Hollywood screen rather cannibalistically had come to accept as behavior. It also inculcated in me a vast desire to work away from the studios, not within the walls of a sound stage. I find a freedom and inspiration from a location that the barren walls of the studio don't give me."[1] In the decades that followed Huston was to prove the sincerity of those remarks as he rarely returned to the sound stages of Hollywood. From the plains of Africa, the coast of Italy, the Egyptian desert, an Irish village, an Austrian meadow, to Stockton, California's skid row, a hallmark of Huston's cinema after the war was the pleasure it took in evoking its setting. The flagrantly studio-bound style of his three prewar features was rarely to be in evidence again. And nowhere was his impatience to be out-of-doors and out-of-Hollywood more obvious than in his very first postwar production. *The Treasure of the Sierra Madre* was, among its other distinctions, probably the first product of a major American studio to be shot almost completely outside the United States.

Scriptwriting Interlude

Huston's return to directing was not immediate however. Upon his discharge from the army, his first stop was the Broadway stage where he directed the American premiere of Jean-Paul Sartre's *Huis Clos* (*No Exit*). Then, back at Warner Brothers (which he found "exactly as I had left it"), he had a hand in writing two excellent thrillers, *The Stranger* (1946), directed by Orson Welles, and *The Killers* (1946), directed by

Huston launches his career of international location shooting in Mexico with The Treasure of the Sierra Madre. *Courtesy of the Museum of Modern Art, Film Stills Archive.*

33

Robert Siodmak. The former was produced by Sam Speigel, later to produce two Huston films, and at first Huston was slated to direct. But Speigel also wanted Orson Welles in the lead role.

Welles, whose directing career was in a slump, made his participation contingent on being allowed to direct as well as act and Speigel reluctantly agreed, though only after seeking to protect himself from Welles's caprices. The contract Welles accepted stipulated that there was to be no deviation from the script Huston had prepared with Anthony Veiller. It was a measure of Welles's desire to live down his reputation as a wild maverick that he agreed. "I did it to prove I could put out a movie as well as anyone else," he stated. And he proved it decisively; there were superb performances by Welles himself, Loretta Young, and Edward G. Robinson, as well as some outlandish camerawork unlikely to have occurred in any Huston-directed film. Huston deserves credit for a fine script, but what reached the screen belonged to Orson Welles.

Huston's second postwar writing project turned into another exemplary film noir. *The Killers* was adapted by Huston from an Ernest Hemingway short story and, again, he was first in line to direct. The obstacle this time was not Welles but a disagreement with producer Mark Hellinger, who eventually chose Robert Siodmak instead. Hellinger, producer of *High Sierra*, knew as much as anyone in Hollywood about making crime films and the film, even without Huston at the helm, proved enormously interesting and was purportedly the only screen adaptation of any of his works of which Hemingway approved. *The Killers* skillfully explored themes of betrayal and sexual enslavement through a curious mélange of expressionistic lighting and camerawork that echoed the style developed at the UFA Studios in prewar Berlin (where Siodmak had worked) with the late forties tendency to stark realism and location shooting. Huston's name, for contractual reasons, did not appear on the credits and he was later to describe his collaborator, Anthony Veiller, as his own "favorite American screenwriter," so again his precise contribution is hard to isolate. All that can be said with certainty about Huston's brief return to the often-anonymous art of screenwriting was that he did it in the very best of company.

The Treasure of the Sierra Madre (1948)

There was no taint of anonymity to the result of his return to the director's chair however; *The Treasure of the Sierra Madre* is often considered the quintessential Huston film. It had in its cast the actor who, since *The Maltese Falcon*, was most associated with Huston, Humphrey Bogart, as well as the director's father, Walter, who was to earn the year's Oscar for Best Supporting Actor. It was Huston's first fiction film to fully exercise his propensity for shooting in exotic locales—Mexico, a land he had always loved and would eventually make his home—and the story was one he chose and adapted personally to the screen. Nor did the studio interfere in the final result: "the film is exactly as I wanted it," he later stated.[2]

Most of all, however, *The Treasure of the Sierra Madre* is considered pure Huston because of its theme. To the degree that a consistent thematic element can be traced through his work (and that degree has often been exaggerated), it concerns the involvement of a band of ill-matched eccentrics in an adventurous quest for something that proves, if not unattainable, certainly not to have been worth the effort necessary to attain it. *The Maltese Falcon* inaugurated the theme, *San Pietro* continued it, and later it was to be woven through at least a dozen Huston works. But *Sierra Madre* distilled the theme to its essence and provided the model against which all subsequent doomed Huston quests were to be measured.

Huston had resolved to bring the story to the screen before the war. It had already been acquired by Warners and would likely have followed *Across the Pacific* if the army had not intervened. Warners' producer Henry Blanke, in an effort for which Huston would remain forever grateful, managed to keep the studio from assigning the property to anyone else while Huston was away so when no directing work grew out of either *The Stranger* or *The Killers*, Huston was ready to tackle the strange adventure tale about gold prospecting.

The author of the original novel, B. Traven, led a life as mysterious and private as Huston's was well documented and public. That he lived and wrote in Mexico was certain, but little else is. Most accounts agree that he was a Bavarian anarchist named Ret Marut who fled Germany in the early twenties and assumed the name "Traum," German for "dream" and an angram for Marut, which was then, accidentally or deliberately, misspelled as Traven. While working on his script, Huston had been in touch with him by letter and had received an exhaustive list of criticisms and suggestions. When he made arrangements to meet with Traven in Mexico City however, the elusive author did not appear. But before Huston returned to California he was contacted by a man who introduced himself as Hal Croves and claimed to be Traven's personal representative, authorized to speak for him on all matters. Suspecting Croves was actually Traven, Huston engaged him as a technical adviser to the production and he was present throughout the shooting.

In the years that followed, as both Huston's film and Traven's books gathered acclaim, the man who had presented himself as Croves willingly admitted that he was Traven. But Huston was not so sure; nothing about either Crove's literary style or his personal manner seemed to him Germanic. Nor did the anarchist activities of Ret Marut seem the work of the timid, retiring Croves. Huston could never reconcile the robust and militantly Marxist character of Traven's writing with the fragile and meticulous traits of the man he met as Croves, a man who struck him as having Scandinavian origins. Years later Huston met Traven's stepdaughter and her description of her father was also at variance with Croves, who was enjoying celebrity as Traven. Huston's final guess was that more than one man had written under the name of Traven, and that Croves may have been one of them.

Another inconsistency in the Croves-as-sole-Traven theory, one never mentioned by Huston, has a direct bearing on his film: there is no evidence that Croves in his role as technical adviser ever voiced any objection to the total removal of the often stridently political qualities of the novel. It is easy to understand why the largely apolitical director, particularly during a period of anticommunist hysteria, would neglect those qualities, but why Traven, the fiery anarchist, would have acquiesced is hard to explain.

Other major elements of the literary source reached the screen intact, however, and perhaps foremost among them was its awe for the savage grandeur of the Mexican landscape that formed an integral part of the drama. Huston had reportedly scouted over eight thousand miles of rugged terrain before settling on the remote locations that, except for just a few sequences shot on a Warners soundstage in Hollywood, were the setting for the entire film. It was as if he wanted the conditions of filmmaking to duplicate those of the prospecting described by Traven: "They toiled like convicts. It was very hot by day and bitterly cold by night. They were high up in the mountains of the Sierra Madre. No road led there, only a mule track as far as the water. The nearest railway station was ten or twelve miles distant by donkey. And to get there you had to go over steep passes, by mountain paths, through water-courses and ravines, along the edges of precipitous cliffs. The whole way there were only a few small Indian villages."[3] Bogart was later to complain in an interview that if Huston "saw a nearby mountain that could serve for photographic purposes, that mountain was not good: too easy to reach. If we could get to a location site without fording a couple of streams and walking through snake-infested areas in the scorching sun, then it wasn't quite right."[4] The rugged terrain appealed to the director back from the front lines in Italy, possessed of his "vast desire to work away from studios." "The only time it's tough to make pictures on location," Huston was quoted as saying, "is when someone is shooting at you."[5]

With just a few exceptions Huston followed the chronology of Traven's book and retained most of its incidents. In one of the first episodes

Traven established the destitution of Dobbs, the character played in the film by Bogart, as well as the condescending charity of the rich; Huston staged the scene as written, but took the liberty of casting himself as the rich American who finally loses patience with Dobbs's begging. The bit role is wonderful for its wit—the director mocking himself by playing the capitalist superior to his proletarian actors—but is also completely faithful to its source. The aptness of characterization is reminiscent of *The Maltese Falcon;* in both cases there is the feeling that the novel's characters were tailored to Huston's specifications.

Another incident a little further on in the tale, also on the subject of the tensions between rich and poor, reveals a divergence between author and filmmaker: Dobbs and Curtin (Tim Holt) have caught up with a crooked labor contractor who owes them money. In both versions they are paid off when they confront him, but not in the same way. In Traven's version, the unscrupulous boss prevails psychologically: he forks over the money while berating his creditors "in the tone one uses in getting rid of importunate beggars for charity." The incident ends with the man walking out on Dobbs and Curtin, "ignoring them as though they had deeply insulted him." For Traven, workers are always scorned and humilated by the bosses when they demand what is rightfully theirs.

Such bowing to an oppressive class system is nowhere present in Huston's version of the same scene. Bogart and Holt act with the manly vigor of the traditional Hollywood Western hero and, appropriately, the sequence was one of the few in the film shot on a Warners set. This time the labor contractor refuses at first to pay and the issue must be resolved with fisticuffs. The fight is portrayed in a scene conspicuous not just for its brutality but for some elaborately subjective camerawork that is unlike any other in the film. One shot is taken from a very low angle, looking up at the villain from the hero's point of view, and recalls an equally unusual subjective shot in *The Maltese Falcon* that framed the threatening mass of Sydney Greenstreet's belly from below. But it is not just cinematic flourish Huston had added to the incident; he has changed it from a comment on class struggle to a piece of straightforward, rowdy action that serves in a most important way to establish a spirit of camaraderie between the two men.

The dissolution of that spirit of camaraderie, its erosion by greed and distrust, is a theme of both book and movie, but in the latter, it is untouched by ideological considerations. For Huston, unlike Traven, it is not the class struggle but the fateful weakness of men's souls alone that destroys the friendship of Dobbs and Curtin. And Huston's most powerful tool in expressing that weakness is an element with which Traven could not have reckoned: the audience's immediate recognition of Bogart as a heroic figure based on their familiarity with his previous

films. The fight scene serves to reinforce an image of the star that had
been established first tentatively in *High Sierra* and then forcefully in
The Maltese Falcon and *Across the Pacific*. After the release of *Casablanca*, Bogart's apotheosis was complete and his two films for Howard
Hawks, *To Have and Have Not* (1944) and *The Big Sleep* (1946), only
cemented it. Viewers knew what to expect: Bogart would be brooding
and ostensibly selfish in the first few reels and then, when push came
to shove, reveal a selfless devotion to all that was righteous and just.
Thus when he and Tim Holt stand up to the bully in the barroom and
use their fists to see that justice is done, Huston perpetuates the Bogart myth and indicates that, despite indications of churlishness, his
gallant nature will reveal itself in the end. When Dobbs and Curtin
follow Howard (Walter Huston) into the mountains, the trio's cooperative spirit seems unshakable. But then they discover gold.

The story's philosophy is, from the beginning, expressed by Howard, but his statement when gold is first discovered is the most oracular
of them all: "finding it ain't all, you got to know how to tickle it, so
she'll come out laughing." The words are not in Traven's book; perhaps
the director's father improvised them on the spot, but in any case, in
a seemingly harmless way, he defines the horror ahead. The gold will
be "tickled" by human treachery and greed and it will "come out laughing." From the moment Huston's camera lingers in closeup on his
expression at the first sight of real gold, Humphrey Bogart was never
to be the same on the movie screen again. The myth of the good "bad
guy" was turned on its head and, to what must have been the astonishment of millions of moviegoers, the hero of *Casablanca* was revealed
as a very bad "good guy," rotten, in fact, to the core. Bogart's slow
degradation, punctuated by such staples of Western action as a confrontation with a deadly Gila monster and a shoot-out with ruthless
bandits, then becomes the film's main concern as it slowly proves how
only the gold itself will "come out laughing."

The idea of laughter as ultimately the only response to the cruelties
of fate figured prominently in the ending of Traven's book as Howard
responded to the expedition's total failure: "He began to laugh so hard
that he had to double up in case he hurt himself. . . . 'If you can't laugh
now till you burst, then you don't know what a good joke is, and that
would be a pity. It's a joke worth ten month's hard labor.' . . . And he
laughed until the tears ran down his cheeks." It might have been that
Huston, in the course of adapting the story to the screen, simply chose
to emphasize the incident for the sake of the drama, but his motivation
likely went deeper.

In January 1937, Walter Huston had starred in an ambitious production of *Othello* on Broadway. In his autobiography, his son remembers the day after its poorly received premiere: "I knew this meant more to my father than anything he had ever done, so, very early in the morning, I took the papers to the Waldorf Towers where he was staying. I went up to his room, and just as I was about to knock, I heard laughter from inside. 'Well,' I thought, 'he won't be laughing when he sees these!' I was glad that at least I would be on hand when he read them. As I entered, I saw the papers strewn over the floor. He was laughing at the reviews! All those years of work and planning that had gone into his *Othello* . . . down the drain! This was to have been his definitive performance. The joke was on him. Pretty soon he had me laughing too" (*OB*, 184)

The kind of affinity that had existed between Hammett and Huston seven years earlier was present between Traven and Huston. "Laugh," says Walter Huston at the film's end, "it's a great joke played on us by the Lord, fate, nature, or whatever you prefer, but whoever, whatever, certainly had a sense of humor." The film's last shot is a closeup of a bag of gold dust lying open on the ground, spewing its contents into the wind. On the soundtrack is laughter. The gold had been tickled until it came out laughing.

Sierra Madre was a rarity among Hollywood films: its location shooting, its absence of love interest, its demolition of the heroic image of a top star, its refusal to tack on a happy ending, all distanced it from the industry's mainstream. Understandably, Warners publicists were uncertain how to promote the work, finally deciding that it was a Western and playing up the idea of a hunt for secret treasure. The public, however, was not fooled and largely spurned the unusually bleak tale. Huston's rewards were not at the box office but in critical esteem; reviewers were unstinting in their praise and Huston won an Oscar for Best Direction to match his father's for Best Supporting Actor. (Bogart was nominated for Best Actor, but lost to Laurence Olivier.) Huston had entered the postwar era, one that was to bring great troubles to the industry as a whole, triumphantly. His stock rose so high that later critics were to become suspicious of the laurels he had earned for *Sierra Madre*. But though the result of his return to fiction filmmaking may have been overpraised, the backlash to that praise does not stand up to close scrutiny. As for the film itself, it continues to pass the test of time spendidly.

Before *Sierra Madre* had been released, and thus before Huston could read in the pages of *Life* that he had just completed "one of the best things Hollywood had done since it learned to talk, a movie that can take its place, without blushing, among the best ever made" (the words were James Agee's),[6] he was already at work on another film. Had he time to bask in the praise that greeted his defiance of Hollywood conventions, he might have balked at ever observing them again. But he was still under contract to Warners and, having allowed him his mad Mexican gallop, they wanted him back in the harness. Producer Jerry Wald assigned Huston the adaptation of an overblown verse drama by Maxwell Anderson.

Key Largo (1948)

Anderson's play dealt with the conscience of a man who had left the safety of America to fight with the Loyalists against Franco's fascist rebels in the Spanish Civil War. In the hills of northern Spain, the man realizes the fight for democracy is futile and urges his comrades to join him in capitulating. They refuse to abandon their ideals and are soon killed; he escapes alive, sinks to abetting the fascists in order to escape, and returns to America. Once home, his act of betrayal haunts him and, in a desperate act of expiation, he travels the country to beg forgiveness from the families of each of his dead friends. His soul-searching journey ends on a remote Florida key where he atones for himself by standing up for two fugitive Indians against a band of crooked gamblers and a corrupt sheriff. The issues of courage and cowardice, loyalty and betrayal, guilt and atonement are not at all veiled in the play; their obviousness is, on the contrary, deafening. The characters' speeches sound very little like natural dialogue and very much like self-conscious poetry. From such material, Huston was asked to make an action-packed but studio-bound melodrama with love interest between Humphrey Bogart and Lauren Bacall and a flamboyant gangster role for the dean of all screen hoodlums, Edward G. Robinson. That he did it must be acknowledged; that it was worth doing need not.

The transition from play to movie began when Huston left Hollywood with writer Richard Brooks for the Florida Keys, presumably convinced that the ambiance of the place itself would aid them even though the play was not that strongly rooted in its locale to begin with. And the pair's changes in the material had little to do with local color. The central motivation of the play's hero, the expiation of his guilt at having deserted his comrades, is demolished at the outset. Perhaps because of studio pressure to restore some nobility to Bogart's screen persona after the tarnish of Sierra Madre, perhaps because the moment seemed inopportune either to evoke the antifascism of the Spanish Civil War or to suggest that any of America's fighting men had ever shirked their duty, the film turned the play's main character into an unblemished hero who arrives in the Keys not to apologize but just to tell the father that his son "was a good soldier." Bogart, who plays the role, suffers from a kind of malaise, but apparently it is not his conscience that bothers him but a kind of general despair about the soul of postwar America.

Humphrey Bogart in two of the confrontations between Huston's "ill-matched eccentrics": (top) with Walter Huston in The Treasure of the Sierra Madre; *(bottom) with Edward G. Robinson as the hoodlum chief Rocco in* Key Largo. *Courtesy of the Museum of Modern Art, Film Stills Archive.*

What Huston substituted for the struggle against fascism in Spain, however, indicates that the change was more than just expedient on his part. In what is one of the truest-sounding and most moving scenes of the film, Bogart recounts his memories of his dead friend to the soldier's father (Lionel Barrymore) and his widow (Lauren Bacall). The setting just happens to be the Italian campaign, the bloody trek north to Rome from Naples. "Once outside San Pietro," Bogart recalls, "he was at a forward observation post . . . others were killed . . . he talked and talked to keep himself awake." Bogart then describes his friend's final resting place: "just crosses on a slope, high up, above the ruins of a church . . . from where George is, you can see a river." The scene is unmistakable; Huston has just literally described images from his own *San Pietro*. The massive casualties, the ruined church, the improvised cemetery, all were in his documentary. Briefly, the plight of Bogart's character becomes totally credible in the context of Huston's war trilogy. He and the dead soldier were among those who had joked around a campfire in *Report from the Aleutians*, one had then survived the battle of San Pietro, the other had not. The survivor shares the plight of the subjects of *Let There Be Light*, asking himself why he lived while all around him died and how he can go on to reintegrate himself into a peacetime society. For a few all too brief moments, *Key Largo* seems to share the concerns of *The Best Years of Our Lives* (1946), a film by another maker of fine war documentaries, William Wyler, that looked honestly at the problems of veterans readjusting to civilian life. But the impression is short-lived; too many other things were crammed into *Key Largo* for it to become the definitive reflection of the war's aftermath, the fictional extension of *Let There Be Light* of which Huston was likely capable.

The burden of Huston's attempt to make a metaphorical statement on the malaise of the late forties rests heavily on the broad shoulders of Edward G. Robinson. The thesis is that after the high idealism of the war years, America was in danger of slipping back into the corrupt ways of the Prohibition era when ruthless gangsters ruled and decent, law-abiding people lived in fear. Those who fought fascism in distant lands must now stand up and defend those same ideals at home. The incarnation of the resurgent evil of the thirties is the actor whose career had been established by the title role in *Little Caesar* (1930), a film that had almost single-handedly established the whole gangster film genre. Offering moviegoers all the vicarious thrills of the luxurious and dangerous lives of the big-time crime chieftans, most notably Al Capone, Robinson became an icon for the cunning and sadistic lords of the underworld. He paid a high price for his instant success—too many of his subsequent roles asked only that he parody his "Little Caesar" character and his true breadth as an actor was not frequently exploited—but it did guarantee him a lifetime of stardom. There were exceptions to the character of the snarling criminal: Billy Wilder's *Double Indemnity* (1944), Fritz Lang's *Scarlet Street* (1946), and the would-be Huston project turned Welles film *The Stranger* notable among them. But when employed by Huston to play the nemesis of Bogart and Bacall, Robinson found himself right back in the *Little Caesar* role of two decades before. In the earlier film he was known as Rico; in the later, Rocco. In both he is violent, sadistic, and contemptuous of the law. The advantage Rico had, though, was that he pretended to be nothing but a successful gangster whereas Rocco's hooliganism has to stand for, as James Agee wrote in his review of the film, "practically everything that is fundamentally wrong with post-war America."[7] The job is simply too demanding even for "the one and only Johnny Rocco."

Still, Robinson has his moments, perhaps the most celebrated being the very first glimpse of him: soaking in a bathtub in a steamy hotel room, a fan directed at his dripping hulk, a newspaper in his hands, and a thick cigar in his mouth. He is, in Huston's words, "a crustacean with its shell off" (*OB*, 151). By the time Robinson rises from the tub, still chomping on his cigar, and wraps himself in a silk bathrobe, his character has been completely defined for anyone who went to American movies in the thirties and forties. The impact of his villainy gave one of his costars, Claire Trevor, the opportunity to win an Oscar. She plays his alcoholic mistress, a washed-up nightclub singer, whom it amuses Rocco to humiliate. Forced by him to give a pathetic rendition of one of her old songs in exchange for a drink, Trevor's Gaye Dawn apparently made the Academy voters so uncomfortable they named her the year's best supporting actress.

But despite the distractions of Robinson's viciousness, Trevor's boozy pathos, Bacall's charm, and a characteristically florid contribution by Lionel Barrymore, the drama ultimately boils down to Bogart playing another variation on his *Casablanca* routine—the "I only look out for myself" cynic transformed, for love of a woman, into a hero full of faith, ideals, and hope for a better world. Just the formula that *Sierra Madre* had so joltingly defied was back in use. The story's finale seems to be a reprise of that of *To Have and Have Not*, with Bogart again the brave skipper of a small boat (a hobby he pursued offscreen). Huston had taken great pleasure in abandoning *Across the Pacific* to another director with Bogart left surrounded by heavily armed Japanese, laughing at how his replacement had contrived a happy ending. But *Key Largo*'s conclusion is just as farfetched as that of the earlier film.

5

Other Wars

IT IS CURIOUS that Huston himself spoke so flippantly of the melodrama of *In This Our Life* and so seriously about that of *Key Largo* when both were no more nor less than well-directed projects undertaken less for personal reasons than because Warners assigned them to him. Still more peculiar, though, was his outright dismissal of the film he made next. He could have excused the heavy-handedness of *Key Largo* by citing that very quality in his literary source. Then he made *We Were Strangers* from his own script and free from studio interference. Inexplicably, he defended the former and disparaged the latter. The fact that it is a far more interesting film than its predecessor could never be inferred from Huston's own comments. The reputation of *We Were Strangers* needs some rehabilitation.

We Were Strangers (1949)

Even before starting *Key Largo* Huston had resolved that it was to be his last picture as a contract director for Warner Brothers. And whether he realized it or not, his impulse to break free of the studio system coincided almost exactly with the beginning of its end. The year after the war ended, 1946, set the all-time record for film industry revenue, but despite the encouraging figures, Hollywood was living on borrowed time. Multiple factors—the advent of television, the baby boom, the demoralizing effects of the anticommunist witch hunts and the blacklist—were all just waiting to do their damage. In the fifties the movie game was either to be played by new rules or played by the old ones with disastrous results. One reason the career of John Huston was to prove so resilient was that, by 1949, he was already observing the new rules.

Sam Spiegel, the producer of *The Stranger*, proposed to Huston a partnership in an independent company to come into being when the director's contract with Warners expired. The concept of independent

Re-creating the Civil War for The Red Badge of Courage.

producing-directing teams that contracted with a major studio for production facilities and distribution services was not Spiegel's invention.
Directors William Wyler, George Stevens, and Frank Capra had pioneered the idea right after the war with their Liberty Films. The fate
of the independent companies was not at first always happy, but they
were to prove the wave of the future. Huston must have sensed this;
he accepted Spiegel's offer and Horizon Pictures was formed. In a rush
to get the company off the ground, they chose as their first project a
short story by Robert Sylvester about Cuban revolutionaries. "It
wasn't a very good choice," Huston wrote later, "and it wasn't a very
good picture" (OB, 163).

If Huston meant "good" in the sense of conventional or profitable,
he was quite right. If he meant it in the sense of imaginative and provocative, he was wrong. Unusual enough was a political subject coming
from an independent company not yet on its feet at a time when the
industry's giants were running scared, terrified that any hint of liberal
sentiment would stir the wrath of right-wing witch hunters in Washington. John Garfield and Jennifer Jones played left-wing guerillas
plotting the overthrow of an oppressive government. There is a quote
from Thomas Jefferson—"Resistance to tyranny is obedience to law"—
and then an instance of tyranny is portrayed: after a summary massacre
of his opponents on the steps of the local university, the Cuban dictator
decides to make assembly of more than four persons a crime. A subservient parliament, one member cowardly following another in the
voting, then unanimously ratifies the law.

Huston had dared to suggest that elected representatives might
choose spiritless acquiescence in the face of a demagogue's attack on
liberty, and he did so not long before an uncannily similar phenomenon occurred between Senator Joseph McCarthy and the United
States Congress. The suggestion was both prophetic and audacious.
Two years earlier the House Committee on Un-American Activities
had singled out the film world as a target in its wide-ranging hunt for
Communist subversives. Huston had been among a group of Hollywood notables to travel to Washington to protest the assault on constitutional rights but the gesture had proved ineffective. Yet, as *We Were
Strangers* decisively proved, he had not, like so many of his colleagues,
been intimidated into avoiding political subjects. In fact, his film had
a most direct parallel to the first manifestations of the McCarthy spirit.

The Smith Act of 1940 was one of the first tools of the Communist-
hunters. Used as a pretext for the prosecution of members of the Communist Party, the law prohibited groups from conspiring to advocate
the violent overthrow of the government. With Thomas Jefferson as
their inspiration, Huston and his script collaborator Peter Viertel made
such a group the heroes of their story. And where there might have

been some ambiguity about the violent intentions of the Americans persecuted by the Smith Act, there was none whatsoever about those of the diehard band headed by Garfield and Jones: their goal was revolution through assassination and sabotage.

Just the sheer audacity of telling such a story in 1949 was impressive. It was one thing to use the tried-and-true cliché of the movie gangster as an incarnation of evil; it was quite another to point a finger at an authoritarian government (and an ally of the United States). The *Hollywood Reporter* was doubtless not alone in its opinion of the film. Calling it "a strange entry for an American motion picture company to put on the market at this time," its reviewer pointed to what he saw as "its blatant propaganda content. It is the heaviest dish of Red theory ever served to an audience outside the Soviet . . . a shameful handbook of Marxian dialectics."[1]

While shooting was not as remote from the studio as *Sierra Madre,* neither is the Cuban setting as patently false as that of the Florida coast in *Key Largo.* Huston went to Cuba to scout locations for second-unit photography that was to be effectively woven into the studio-shot scenes involving the major cast members. Since the ostensible subject of the story was a popular uprising in 1933 against a widely hated dictator, the current Cuban government was cooperative and assigned a "cultural advisor" to the project, a professor from the University of Havana. Yet Huston (and perhaps, secretly, his "cultural advisor" as well) was under no illusion that the present regime was any better than the one his protagonists were trying to overthrow. "All the conditions in Cuba certainly indicated that a revolution was required," Huston said later. "It was, at the time, just about as corrupt a place as there was in my experience of the world. . . . I think what happened in Cuba can be laid directly at the door of the United States, especially the industrialists, and sugar and fruit plantation owners."[2] If the conservative press was upset about *We Were Strangers* in 1949, their reaction had it been released a decade later, as Fidel Castro's revolution triumphed, can easily be imagined.

The film is by no means without its flaws. Huston himself was particularly uncomfortable with the idea of all of the Cubans in it speaking English. And the romantic struggles of the revolutionaries, particularly as presented by a seductive-looking Jennifer Jones, are not without falsely melodramatic moments. But there is compensation for the weaknesses in the genuine spirit of shared struggle within the revolutionary group and their desperate mission. The digging of a tunnel into a cemetery, to get them close to a funeral attended by high government officials, is conveyed with great suspense. The group's work is sweaty, frantic, and claustrophobic to begin with. Then, as their tunnel reaches the cemetery and, near exhaustion, they have to wear masks to avoid succumbing to the stench of buried corpses, it becomes truly nightmarish—a vision of hell.

We Were Strangers has some of the film noir toughness of *The Maltese Falcon* combined with the sense of tropical heat that Huston had used in virtually all of his films to that date. *In This Our Life* was set in the American Deep South, *Across the Pacific* in Panama, *Sierra Madre* in Mexico, *Key Largo* in the Florida Keys, and now Huston was in Cuba. Always the heat had given his films an explosive quality, but seldom was the explosion as literal as the one that rocks Havana. When the group's quest fails, there is no ironic laughter in the *Sierra Madre* manner, but instead a rekindling of the action. A machine-gun battle begins in earnest as the police close in on Garfield and Jones and the screen goes literally white with gunfire and dynamite. Garfield dies a martyr's death that accomplishes what he could not do in life: it sparks a revolution. The tale may be a bit farfetched, but it is consistently exciting. And given the timing of its release, it's as if Huston had deliberately sought to toss a Molotov cocktail in the form of a movie at the reactionary political leadership of the day.

In and Out of *Quo Vadis*

Huston's commercial fortunes reached a nadir after *We Were Strangers* was released to a spectrum of response that ranged from hostility to indifference. Spiegel and Huston judged it prudent not to push ahead immediately with another independent production. The time was ripe for Huston to retreat from risky small projects and re-establish himself with a safe and lavish conventional one. The pattern of directors taking refuge in tried-and-true formulas after an unhappy experiment was not uncommon; Alfred Hitchcock often spoke of "running for cover" to sure-fire material when he needed to rebuild his box office power. Huston at the time looked poised to do just that when he signed a contract with the most bourgeois of studios, Metro-Goldwyn-Mayer, and started preparations on *Quo Vadis*. Louis B. Mayer, the aggressively middlebrow head of the studio, saw the story of persecuted Christians in ancient Rome as offering the avantages of a Cecil B. DeMille epic: viewers could revel in the decadence of pagan hedonism while pretending to condemn it. It was the kind of hypocrisy that could not have been more alien to Huston's temperament. But a Hollywood director, particularly one deeply in debt, often had to swallow his pride and take what was offered him.

Perhaps Huston would have found a way to handle *Quo Vadis* in a way that would have both pleased Louis B. Mayer and preserved his own integrity, but it does not seem likely. Luckily, he never had to try. After the film had been cast and preproduction work begun in Rome (but before Huston and Mayer came to an agreement on the script), Gregory Peck, slated for the lead role, developed an eye infection and the production was delayed. The postponement allowed Huston to switch to a project for which he was ideally suited and to let the gargantuan epic pass into the anonymous hands of director Mervyn LeRoy. Mayer got the *Quo Vadis* he wanted and Huston made what is often considered his finest film.

The Asphalt Jungle (1950)

The elements that had congealed so seamlessly in *The Maltese Falcon* and *Sierra Madre* came together again: Huston's temperament, his cast's talents, and the power of a perfectly suited literary source. What Huston had brought to the work of Dashiell Hammett and B. Traven, he now brought to that of W. R. Burnett. The ensemble acting he had drawn first from Bogart, Mary Astor, Peter Lorre, and Sydney Greenstreet, and then from Bogart, Tim Holt, and his own father, he now found in Sterling Hayden, Louis Calhern, and Sam Jaffe. The movie was *The Asphalt Jungle*.

Huston had already, of course, had some happy experiences with bringing Burnett's work to the screen. One of his first attempts at screenwriting had been from a Burnett story, a film starring Walter Huston, *Law and Order*. And almost a decade later, it was with Burnett material that Huston opened the door to a directing career through Raoul Walsh's *High Sierra*. In a sense, Burnett's spirit had also hovered over *Key Largo*, for, as the author of *Little Caesar*, he had created Edward G. Robinson's character, Rico, whom Huston had turned into Rocco. So working from a Burnett source for the first time as a director, Huston had every reason to be sure of himself and trust to an approach that had already served him well: stick close to the book. And this time he went a step further; before shooting began Huston took his script to Burnett for advice and approval.

Huston had no comparable previous acquaintance with his cast— they were primarily contract players at MGM and it was his first film at that studio—but he was no less well served. The choice of Sam Jaffe as a timid criminal mastermind obsessed by young women and of Louis Calhern as a suavely evil lawyer were natural ones, but Huston had to fight with MGM Production Chief Dore Schary to get his choice for the film's most important role, Sterling Hayden. "They just don't know what to make of a guy like you in this business," Huston is reported to have told Hayden when they first met.[3] But *The Asphalt Jungle* was soon to show exactly "what to make of a guy" like Hayden.

What Huston was referring to was Hayden's volatile demeanor. It was not just his physically intimidating size; he also had an air of being capable of violence. Hayden's face expressed an intelligence and sensitivity that made his physical force more threatening. There were obviously contradictory impulses raging inside him that came through forcefully on the movie screen but were evidently unnerving to his employers. The fact that he was waging a losing war against alcoholism only heightened the sense of menace.

Hayden is introduced in Huston's film amid a setting with the quintessential ambience of the film noir. There is a wasteland of train tracks, desolate-looking warehouses, dingy oil storage tanks, and grimy alleys full of rubble. Soon there is visible the pathetic facade of a little café that could have been the subject of a melancholy painting by Edward Hopper or a Depression-era photograph by Walker Evans or Bernice Abbott. Inside the forlorn diner, Hayden is peremptorily arrested and hauled down to a police station. There, lined up with other unsavory detainees, he taciturnly offers almost all of the information the viewer will ever have about him: "Age: 36. Born: Kentucky. Profession: None." Hayden has been arrested for robbery but his victim, when suddenly face-to-face with his sullen presence, is afraid to identify him. The mood has been set and for the next one hundred minutes, Huston will maintain it perfectly.

In a dangerous-looking neighborhood, down a dark hallway, lives "the professor" (Sam Jaffe), a mousy little man who has the brains to conceive ambitious robberies but who needs help with the muscle. That, in the jungle of asphalt, is not hard to find. Besides the titanic Hayden, there is an avaricious bookie (Marc Lawrence, who had been Robinson's malevolent side-kick in *Key Largo*), a surly hunchback (James Whitmore), a devoted family man skilled at safecracking (Anthony Caruso), a corrupt cop (Barry Kelley), and a nightclub floozy (Jean Hagen), in short, a broadly representative sample of the lower depths of big city life. It is a society whose members offer the toast: "Here's to the drink habit—the only one I got that don't get me into trouble."

Looming above it all in a financial sense but, if possible, below it all in a moral one, is a reptilian lawyer (Louis Calhern) whose wealth allows him to bankroll crimes and afford a frivolous blond plaything. That plaything occupies a relatively minor position in the drama in terms of time on the screen, but her impact both on this film and the industry as a whole was major. She is Marilyn Monroe. Although under contract to 20th Century-Fox, Monroe had not yet had a speaking role in a film when Huston selected her to be Calhern's feather-brained mistress. Fox, in fact, had already decided to drop their option to renew her contract. When they saw *The Asphalt Jungle*, they quickly changed their minds.

*Mastermind Louis Calhern (second from right) dominates a typically tense scene in
Huston's film noir* The Asphalt Jungle. *Courtesy of the Museum of Modern Art,
Film Stills Archive.*

Monroe is first glimpsed curled up on a couch in Calhern's luxurious
apartment; the camera lingers on the line of her thigh. As Calhern
sends her off to the bedroom so she won't be exposed to the ugly details of his loan-sharking business, he refers to her as "some sweet kid,"
a remark echoed two years later in Howard Hawks's fine screwball
comedy, *Monkey Business* (1952), when Cary Grant describes her as
"half-child, but not the half that shows." Calhern's evident pleasure at,
as a disapproving rival puts it, "consorting with a girl young enough to
be his granddaughter" was to be duplicated by various males in virtually every film the actress was to make. Her combination of juvenile
volubility with thoroughly adult physical charms was exploited again
and again, but Huston was the first to discover the possibility.

"Am I excited! Yikes!" Monroe squeals when Calhern shows her a
glossy travel brochure about Cuba, where he has promised to take her.
The sequence is rich in associations because, besides defining Monroe's screen persona, it refers back to the setting of *We Were
Strangers*—the bloody tyranny beneath the veneer of holiday merri-

ment. And perhaps director Francis Ford Coppola remembered the
scene when he brilliantly evoked Cuba, the refuge of American crime
lords, on the eve of revolution in *The Godfather, Part II* (1974). In any
case, when Lee Strasberg in the latter film closes the door on his wife
so that she will not hear his criminal negotiations with Al Pacino, he
almost duplicates Calhern's gesture a quarter century earlier. Marilyn
Monroe could have asked for no better debut.

The film's dialogue seems to grow naturally out of the grubby streets
and greasy cafés and provides a virtual lexicon of low-life wisdom:
"Hooligans—they're just like left-handed pitchers, all have a screw
loose somewhere." "I can smell a cop a mile away." "You can't trust a
cop, just when you depend on him, he turns out to be legit." "I shudda
been in the money years ago." And the soundest piece of advice of all:
"If ya want fresh air, don't look for it in this town." The words are
hammered out relentlessly, reinforcing the nervous tension of the
criminal's mission.

Though it had many imitators, Huston's tale of (as it describes itself)
"the biggest caper ever to be pulled in the Midwest" stands above
them. With the personalities of its eccentric characters well established, *The Asphalt Jungle* details the mechanics of a crime. Hayden's
huge, brutish fist encloses a tiny bottle of nitroglycerin. The camera
tracks down an underground pipe shaft, following the protagonists, and
the explosive is set with the premonitory comment, "It's gonna take a
lot to blow this baby." Suddenly the break-in triggers a hidden alarm
and the whole surrounding neighborhood is screeching with police si-
rens. With their adversaries closing in, the thieves show grace under
pressure and, refusing to be hurried, complete their job and crawl
away through a sewer. The critical point in the classic early Huston
film has been reached.

In *The Maltese Falcon*, it is the point where Bogart finally thinks he
is in possession of the black bird. In *San Pietro*, it is when American
soldiers finally reach the hilltop village. In *Sierra Madre*, it is when
Bogart, Holt, and Walter Huston have found and mined their gold.
And when Garfield and Jones complete their tunnel into the cemetery,
the moment has come in *We Were Strangers*. It is the moment when
what should have been exultant triumph is suddenly marred by un-
foreseen ambiguities and complications. The bird is not genuine, the
hill may not have been worth taking, the gold corrodes the human
bonds necessary for survival, the assassination target's plans have
changed, making the tunnel pointless. In *The Asphalt Jungle*, the
thieves have escaped with their loot, but it turns out that Calhern,
who was supposed to buy the stolen jewels, is in fact bankrupt and
planning a double cross. There is a series of quick cuts between close-
ups of the sweating faces of the desperate men. The expertly executed

crime gives way to a chaotic aftermath; the band, unified in its work, unravels while the police close in.

That criminals should get their just comeuppance in the end was required by the Production Code authorities. But though Huston's film technically complies with those standards, there is not a whiff of moral superiority to those who enforce the law. The city's police commissioner seems a nasty, mean-spirited character and his temperament affects his underlings. "The commissioner's mad," says a police lieutenant to explain his brutal treatment of a suspect, "he's out for blood and it's not gonna be mine." By contrast, Hayden's character, ostensibly a killer, seems noble: his calm under pressure, his steadfast loyalty to his partners, and his nostalgic dream of returning to his roots in the Kentucky bluegrass where he can "get the city dirt off," all make him far more appealing than any other character. And it is the mortally wounded Hayden's doomed effort to regain his dream of Eden in the form of a horse farm that forms the film's affecting denouement. "He hasn't got enough blood in him to keep a chicken alive," remarks the doctor who examines him, but Hayden struggles on into Kentucky. As the arrogantly victorious police commissioner praises himself to the media ("Suppose we had no police force, then the jungle wins, the predatory beasts take over"), and describes the prey they are seeking ("a man without human feeling or human mercy"), the subject in question reaches the gently rolling hills he so much loves. Behind the neat white fences surrounding a rich bluegrass field and peaceful farm pond, with regal thoroughbreds gamboling around him, the "predatory beast" finds his final resting place. He, more than the police who pursued him, knew enough about the underbelly of urban America to realize "if ya want fresh air, don't look for it in this town." John Huston had made a masterpiece of film noir.

The Red Badge of Courage (1951)

Improbably, after the bleakest of "black films," the career of John Huston continued at the citadel of wholesome family entertainment, Metro-Goldwyn-Mayer. That the studio kept him working in a vein totally contrary to its own proclaimed standards was perhaps as good an indication as any that it was drifting without a rudder. *The Asphalt Jungle*, studio chief Louis B. Mayer is reported to have said, "is full of nasty, ugly people doing nasty, ugly things. I wouldn't walk across the room to see a thing like that."[4] Yet Huston's next project for the studio, *The Red Badge of Courage*, was one that, if anything, Mayer liked even less. Later the seemingly inexplicable phenomenon of a studio producing films its own leader detested became explainable: Mayer was locked in a power struggle with the studio's vice-president in charge of production, Dore Schary, and it was in Mayer's interest to defer to Schary on a project—especially if he thought its failure would weaken Schary's position. Mayer was the ultimate loser in the struggle, as Schary secured the backing of Nicholas Schenk, the president of MGM's parent company, Loew's Incorporated. In the process, Huston's second film for the studio was taken out of his hands and altered until it pleased no one. But what remained still bears the traces of Huston's talent and, if a failure, holds more interest than most of what, in the Hollywood of the early fifties, was deemed successful.

The reputation of *The Red Badge of Courage* has, in the years since its release, suffered from a handicap that proved more debilitating than MGM's interference: it was the subject of what was, in the words of a reviewer for *Newsweek* magazine, "the best book on Hollywood ever published."[5] Called simply *Picture*, the account of the making of Huston's eighth feature film was written by a reporter for the *New Yorker* magazine, Lillian Ross. Later the practice of issuing a book on "the making of" a given film was to become a promotional technique with the book's release carefully coordinated with that of its subject. But Ross's account was no publicist's gimmick; it took an acerbic view of its subject that had the effect of making the film seem worse than it was. Appearing first as a series of articles in the *New Yorker* and then in book form, Ross's material undoubtedly reached a far greater audience than did Huston's film, which, written off as a failure by MGM even before its release, received only cursory distribution.

In Ross's book, the hero among the production's participants, whose characters she delineates in novelistic fashion, is its producer, Gottfried Reinhardt. As an MGM staff producer, Reinhardt, the son of the great theatrical director Max Reinhardt, was responsible for overseeing all of the financial details of the film, mediating between the studio and Huston and trying to give him the freedom to get his vision of Stephen Crane's Civil War novel onto the screen. By Ross's description, Reinhardt was a man of immense taste, integrity, and devotion to the project (all qualities she was reluctant to attribute in too great a measure to Huston), and, if the film could have been a masterpiece, it was through his efforts alone.

Huston is presented as a colorful, rambunctious character with a rather short attention span and a somewhat irresponsible attitude toward his work. *Picture* concludes by describing an embattled Reinhardt struggling on against hopeless odds as MGM ruthlessly disemboweled and cheapened the film he so believed in. The carefree Huston, on the other hand, was off cavorting in Africa shooting his next film, blithely unconcerned about the fate of his last one.

Ross's facts prove conclusively that *The Red Badge of Courage* was an artistic disaster. The studio had made changes in it against Huston and Reinhardt's will. But what is not mentioned is that they are no more obvious to the viewer than the fact that Huston did not direct the last scene of *Across the Pacific*. Without Ross's book, the prevailing critical opinion of the film would no doubt have remained that of its first reviewers who called it "one of the best war films ever made" that caught "brilliantly and unforgettably the great drama of that far-flung battle between brothers" with a cast who were "all first rate and give a vivid sense of bewildered men caught in a cruel moment of history," in short "a classic of American twentieth century filmmaking."[6] The disparity between Ross's account of a failure and the critics' admiration for a success raises the possibility that the production of any Hollywood film might seem like the victory of Philistinism over high art if the process were scrutinized closely enough.

Another problem with Ross's seemingly definitive analysis is her view of the role of the production's director. Reinhardt felt that Huston had abdicated his responsibilities by not staying to fight against changes in the film and he wrote a reproachful letter to him in Africa implying that he cared more for Huston's art than Huston did: "Maybe I have a special idea of a John Huston picture. Maybe even more special than John Huston has."[7] Not surprisingly, Reinhardt turned from producing to directing after his unhappy experience with Huston. But the results belie the suggestion that he had a gift for direction. And though Ross was offended that those who favorably commented on Huston's film were wrong not to credit its producer, Reinhardt's contributions were obviously limited to defending Huston's final version of the film against Dore Schary's changes. But since Schary had final authority over everything the studio released, he overruled Reinhardt. The film had been finished to Huston's satisfaction when he left for Africa. His choice had been whether to go on to a new work or stay behind to fight battles he would most likely lose over a completed one. By choosing the former, he became the villain of *Picture*.

But the images that actually reached the screen, however their length and order may have been modified, belonged to the film's director, and the reviewers of the day had every reason to speak of a "John Huston film." Huston was not happy over the deletions Schary made, but what survived was still his. He had wanted the photography to have something of the look of Matthew Brady's photographic documents of the Civil War and, with cinematographer Harold Rosson, he realized that goal. He had wanted to make the film without big-name stars, without any sentimental love interest (indeed without any major female roles at all) and he did. Huston had wanted actors who had strong, unique personalities, but who were not movie-world celebrities already identified with other roles. In Audie Murphy, the most decorated soldier of World War II, political cartoonist Bill Mauldin, and character actors John Dierkes, Royal Dano, and Arthur Hunnicutt, he succeeded at that as well. Above all, it had been Huston's desire to bring to the spirit of Stephen Crane the same fidelity he had brought to the work of Hammett, Traven, and Burnett. And that was a problem that finally had little to do with Reinhardt, Schary, and MGM.

The problem was that of language. Crane, like Hammett and Burnett, had made a scrupulous effort to make his characters speak the dialect of their milieu. For the latter two, that had just meant weaving a bit of current underworld slang into their dialogue. But for Crane, who was himself trying to re-create events that happened three decades before he started writing, it meant sometimes almost incomprehensible rural accents. After battle, a soldier remembers: "I was talkin' 'cross pickets with a boy from Georgie, onct, an' that boy, he ses, 'Your fellers 'll all run like hell when they onct hearn a gun,' he ses. 'Mebbe they will,' I ses, 'but I don't b'lieve none of it,' I ses; 'an' b'jiminey,' I ses back t' 'um, 'mebber your fellers 'll all run like hell when they onct hearn a gun,' I ses. He larfed. Well, they didn't run t' day, did they, hey? No sir! They fit, an' fit, an' fit." Given the inexact nature of capturing the sound of dialect on paper, it's unlikely that Crane himself could have read such a speech convincingly. So it was not surprising that Huston's actors had, to quote from *Life* magazine's favorable review, "trouble getting their 20th Century mouths around the archaic expletives."[8] Huston, in fact, took less dialogue directly from his literary source than he had in his earlier adaptations, and instead depended on his own well-tuned ear to write lines that would find a middle ground between the inauthentic and the unpronounceable.

The question of Huston's loyalty to Crane's themes, however, is certainly the most important, and here the judgment is simpler. Crane's work is about the nature of cowardice and courage and the hazy boundaries between the two during organized warfare. It is about the mentality of men in the presence of death and how the instinct of self-preservation collides with the notion of duty to an abstract cause. It is about guilt, humiliation, pride, self-respect, fear, and aggression. It is a moral inquiry into the idea of redemption through trial-by-fire. That these issues were of real interest to John Huston is clear from his films.

The peculiar moral code of Sam Spade in *The Maltese Falcon* ("When a man's partner is killed, he's supposed to do something about it."), the deterioration of men's characters under violent stress in *Sierra Madre*, the moral preachments of *Key Largo* ("Better to be a live coward, than a dead hero," says Claire Trevor to an uncertain Bogart), and the study of the individual's duty to act in response to Jefferson's axiom that "resistance to tyrants is obedience to law" in *We Were Strangers*, as well as Sterling Hayden's composure in the face of danger and loyalty to his partners in *The Asphalt Jungle*—all were related in certain ways to the themes of Crane's novel. But as direct as those connections are, they pale in comparison to the rapport between *The Red Badge of Courage* and Huston's war trilogy.

The depth of Huston's feeling for Crane's story may perhaps be gauged by his statement after completing *Let There Be Light* that no matter how many times he was asked to make a war film, "I could never bring myself to film any." His study of the war's effect on men's spirits was for him the last word. "If there was a war picture to be made, that was the time to do it, rather than on a back lot or a fake location."[9] Yet here, six years later, was Huston doing just what he had vowed not to do: shoot a fictional war story on a "fake location." The reason could only have been that in Crane's novel Huston had found something that deepened and validated the message of his war trilogy. The parallels are uncanny: the uncertainty and impatience of untried soldiers in the first part of Crane's book correspond to that pictured in *Report from the Aleutians*. The horror of actual combat that Crane describes later is captured by Huston in *San Pietro*, and, finally, the inquiry into what happens to a man's spirit after exposure to such combat that is the novel's central subject is likewise that of *Let There Be Light*. It was as if Huston had already made a documentary version of *The Red Badge of Courage*.

The manner in which Huston staged his re-creation of the Civil War may not have been the most spectacular in film history (that honor may forever belong to the first great epic of the screen, D. W. Griffith's *The Birth of a Nation* [1915]), but it was nonetheless impressive. His first wish had been to shoot on location where the war had actually been fought; he had a site in mind in Leesburg, Virginia. Then while on a horse-buying trip to Kentucky, he found a location near Nashville that he felt would suit his purposes even better. Finally he settled on a less ambitious (and, for MGM, cheaper) site: his own ranch in the San Fernando Valley, not far from Hollywood. Literally in his own backyard and on an only slightly more distant location on the Sacramento River near Chico, California, Huston was able to capture and maintain an air of total authenticity.

The director's first idea had been to direct the film on horseback. He was forced to abandon it (too hard on the horse, he claimed), but the feeling of nineteenth-century cavalry maneuvers remained. There are numerous impressive views of troops deploying against rolling hills, drilling on open fields, fording broad rivers, and marching through dense woods as cannon fire booms in the distance. Clouds of dust rise from the passage of galloping horses; the figures of men scurrying to avoid the bombardment of exploding shells, each throwing up a little storm of dirt and debris as it collides with the ground. In one extraordinary shot, Rosson's camera captures several isolated combat-

ants beneath some towering trees. The scene is back-lit with the sun
illuminating the dust and smoke of battle in a ghostly way, providing
visual confirmation for a soldier's observation that "men look much
bigger through the powder smoke." On the soundtrack is a pounding
mélange of martial music and the sounds of battle: furious yells, bugles
blowing, rifles crackling, and cannons blasting. Through it all walks
Audie Murphy looking exactly as if he were feeling what Crane described as "the effects of the war atmosphere—a blistering sweat, a
sensation that his eyeballs were about to crack like hot stones. A burning roar filled his ears."

Murphy had never had a major film role before, nor, as it turned
out, was he ever to have another as important. His sole distinction was
his combat record and, by his own admission, his performance was
heavily dependent upon Huston's coaching. Murphy was from a family
of Texas sharecroppers, one of nine children, abandoned by their father when he was fourteen, their mother dead when he was sixteen.
Shortly afterward, he had tried to enlist in the marines and was rejected as underweight. Finally the army accepted him and he became
its most celebrated recruit, winning more medals than any other soldier. Huston was fascinated with his seemingly contradictory mixture
of youthful innocence and near-suicidal bravery in combat—"a gentle
little killer," he called him. There was a combination of adolescent na-
ïveté with a knowledge of the most horrific experiences—a combination that had also been visible in the faces of many of the young
veterans Huston had interviewed in *Let There Be Light*. Murphy's face
helped establish the essential tone of the film.

And tone, more than a clear-cut sequential narrative, is what most
distinguished Huston's version of Crane's novel. Although the studio
tried various means of rearranging the film's scenes to give it a simpler,
more comprehensible narrative line, no amount of tinkering could provide what Huston had not put there to begin with. "The way the picture plays now," Ross quoted Dore Schary as saying to Reinhardt
shortly after Huston had left for Africa, "it's got no story."[10] There followed several unavailing months of effort to concoct one, but Huston
had left the most traditional of studios with a film that was resolutely
unorthodox. Decades later, mood and character studies were to become common movie fare and it became acceptable to eschew a
straight story line, but at MGM in 1951 it was not. Huston had combined a meditation on cowardice and courage with a vivid sense of the
actual conditions of infantry warfare in the Civil War. He had been
loyal to the genius of Stephen Crane.

6

After Hollywood

AT THE END OF 1951 John Huston was the darling of those in the intellectual world who detested Hollywood. His credentials were impeccable: after finishing the war with a documentary banned by the army, his every effort, with the single exception of *Key Largo*, had avoided a happy ending, been spurned by the public, and thereby lost money at the box office. His work had proved by his unpopularity that he was no lowly hack pandering to popular tastes, but was indeed a "serious artist."

Sierra Madre had been the anti-Hollywood film par excellence. Critic Gilbert Seldes had praised it for being "virtually disowned by Warner Brothers" (actually the studio, after all the Oscars, was probably quite proud of the film), and he went on to say that "it had a rare austerity; everything that could make it popular was excluded—to make way for everything that made it magnificent." Having established the polarity between the "popular" and the "magnificent," Seldes regretfully announced that Huston had now chosen the former. In an attempt to curry favor with the ignorant masses, Huston had sunk to making a "low comedy" that "never tries to be important" and was "without depth or distinction."[1] Huston's fall from grace was caused by *The African Queen*.

The African Queen (1952)

An ironic aspect to Huston's descent from the pedestal of high art was the fact that with him went one of those most responsible for hoisting him onto it. The screenplay of *The African Queen*, which was adapted from the novel of the same name by C. S. Forester, was coauthored by James Agee. Little more than a year earlier Agee, in a profile of Huston in *Life* called "Undirectable Director," had proclaimed him "the most inventive director of his generation . . . magnanimous, disinterested and fearless" and one who had "done more to extend, invigorate and purify the essential idiom of American movies, the truly

Memorable confrontations: (top) Humphrey Bogart and Katharine Hepburn in The African Queen; *(bottom) Jose Ferrer as artist Henri de Toulouse-Lautrec, and his mother (Claude Nollier) in* Moulin Rouge. *Courtesy of the Museum of Modern Art, Film Stills Archive.*

visual telling of stories, than anyone since the prime of
D. W. Griffith."[2] Agee's article had led to a meeting with Huston, the
two became friends, and Agee had spoken of his desire to write for the
screen. While Huston was shooting *The Red Badge of Courage*, Agee
wrote a screen adaptation of Crane's short story *The Blue Hotel* with
the vague understanding that it would be Huston's next project. Unfortunately it was not—the disastrous commercial fortunes of the first
Crane-Huston combination precluded a second. But Huston was im-
pressed with Agee's script nonetheless and when pressed by producer
Sam Spiegel to get to work on a script from the Forester story, Huston
arranged for Agee to join him in California to collaborate.

The failure of *We Were Strangers* had apparently not dampened the
enthusiasm of the resourceful Spiegel for either independent production or partnership with Huston. Even while Gottfried Reinhardt was
trying to keep his "undirectable director's" attention focused on the
editing of his Civil War story, Spiegel was pushing for Huston to start
a script from a property he had purchased from 20th Century-Fox.
Spiegel's practice was to try to unearth stories the major studios owned
but had never used, then talk them into selling him the rights for a
minimum of cash in advance and a percentage of future profits if the
project was successful. Forester's adventure tale was just such material. Published in 1935, before its author had gained widespread fame
with his stories about an English sailor named Hornblower, *The African Queen* had been first purchased by Warner Brothers and slated for
filming in 1938, with David Niven in the role of a slovenly Cockney
riverboat skipper and Bette Davis as the prim missionary who falls in
love with him. The film was to follow the couple on a death-defying
adventure down an African river. The idea of the suave Niven as an
uncouth drunkard and the sensuous Davis as a repressed spinster,
however, sounds ill-conceived and apparently someone realized as
much, for the project never materialized. Eight years later, Warners
attempted to resurrect the property, this time with an even less char-
ismatic combination of Paul Henreid and Ida Lupino. Saner heads
must again have prevailed for production plans were once again abandoned, and the story was sold to Fox. After another five years, Spiegel
acquired it from them and put together the most promising of all the
proposed star pairings—Humphrey Bogart and Katharine Hepburn.

In its original form, the story seemed to fit neatly into the Huston
formula of eccentric characters embarked on an ambitious quest that
was doomed from the start. Forester had his unlikely pair of lovers
attempting to navigate a thirty-foot steam launch down an unnavigable
African river, every mile of which was impeded by life-threatening
hazards. Their goal was the destruction of a German gunboat whose
presence on the great lake into which the river emptied gave its com-

manders control of central Africa during World War I. It was a mission as outlandish as the recovery of a priceless ancient artifact by a private eye in San Francisco or the liberation of Cuba by an eccentric American digging a tunnel into a cemetery. And Forester had put the ultimate Huston stamp on his story: the mission of the Cockney and the spinster ended in failure.

Huston and Agee began their writing in the same spirit of fidelity to their literary source that had served the director so well. Little evidence of Agee's unique sensibility was apparent nor any basic change in Huston's impulses; their script was simply a condensation of Forester's book, slightly modified to meet the demands of another medium. Nor did Huston's determination to shoot much of the film on remote locations in central Africa represent a change in his methods. In fact if the rigors of the Sierra Madre had made his telling of Traven's story bleaker and more harrowing, the African setting should have made his recounting of Forester's tale even more so. As he had for the Mexican film, Huston began by scouting thousands of miles of territory by plane. He was looking for a wild jungle river and whenever, in his flights over Uganda, Rhodesia (now Zimbabwe), and the Belgian Congo (now Zaire), he saw a promising one, his small plane would put down in the nearest clearing and his search would continue by canoe. He eventually settled on the Ruiki, a tributary of the Congo River in the Belgian Congo and made his production headquarters at Ponthierville (now Kindu), a cargo depot where river traffic had to be unloaded to get around an impassable stretch before continuing downstream to Lake Albert. Here was constructed a small compound of temporary buildings to house cast, crew, and equipment. Huston had arranged for shooting conditions that would make those of *Sierra Madre* seem like Hollywood luxury.

Determining the exact purpose served by choosing such an incommodious location makes for interesting speculation. It had, of course, its publicity value—the juxtaposition of movie world glamor with wilderness squalor. There was also the advantage of authenticity in the setting as well as the possibility that its director would, as he had stated right after the war, "find a freedom and an inspiration from a location that the barren walls of the studio don't give me."[3] But another element that cannot be completely counted out was less noble: Huston was clearly in love with the manly Hemingway image of the big game hunter and wanted to be in Africa for the sport of it all.

Two arguments can be made that *The African Queen* might just as well have been shot primarily in a studio with a second unit dispatched in Africa to shoot background material (as had been done with the Florida Keys in *Key Largo* and Cuba in *We Were Strangers*). The first is that those scenes that were shot in a tank at the Isleworth Studios near

London are indistinguishable from the location material. The second is that the film ended up being marred by studio artifice anyway; in one particularly awkward section, scenes of what are all-too-obviously two dummies dressed up to look like Bogart and Hepburn careening down treacherous rapids are juxtaposed with shots of the two stars performing against an equally obvious back-projection screen filled with scenes of a wild river.

But a still more persuasive argument for not having bothered with real jungle was the nature of the story itself. Unlike *Sierra Madre*, where the desolate terrain became an objective correlative for the desolation of the characters' souls, *The African Queen* takes on a comic tone quite independent in spirit from its savage setting. Forester's tale had been a love story as well as a rousing adventure, and there was a comic undertone to the account of a spinster missionary becoming aware of her sexuality when thrown into life-and-death circumstances with a Cockney ne'er-do-well: "And no woman with Rose's upbringing could live for ten days in a small boat with a man—even a man like Allnutt—without broadening her ideas and smoothing away the jagged corners and making of her something more like a human being." Huston took full advantage of the peculiar chemistry that developed between Bogart and Hepburn and chose to play up the budding romance between the two. The result would surely have been just as easy to pursue on a studio soundstage. Huston said later that "with Bogie, it wasn't so much where you acted but how you acted, and he'd just as soon have been at home" (*OB*, 203).

The comic tone was established at the very beginning of the film by the personality of an actor who would surely never have considered going to Africa (his scenes were all shot in the London studio), Robert Morley. In Forester's book, his character, the heroine's missionary brother, dies within the first paragraphs. In the film he has plenty of time to exploit the opportunities of playing the pompous snob opposite Bogart's unassuming bum. The comedy begins at once as the natives Morley has been trying to Christianize show more interest in Bogart's discarded cigar butt than in their pastor's church service. Then Huston goes for belly laughs in a quite literal sense: Morley, serving high tea, glares imperiously at the hapless Bogart, who cannot keep his stomach from rumbling.

Aside from a change in the hero's nationality from English to Canadian so as to be spared the probably impossible task of imitating a heavy Cockney accent, Bogart adapted himself extremely well to Forester's Charlie Allnutt, the pitiable slum-bred boat mechanic who had ended up in Africa, never having been "sufficiently self-analytical to appreciate that most of the troubles of his life resulted from attempts to avoid trouble." Hepburn's character, Rose Sayer, however, required considerable modification to fit the actress's range and that proved yet another element in the drift of the material toward comedy. Forester's Rose had never known romance; but physically, despite languishing during her twenties at her brother's isolated mission, her early thirties body was ready to bloom: "Those big breasts of hers, which had begun to sag when she had begun to lapse into spinsterhood, were firm and upstanding now again, and she could look down at them swelling out the bosom of her white drill frock without misgiving. Even in these ten days her body had done much toward replacing fat where fat should be and eliminating it from those areas where it should not."

In addition to her obvious anatomical dissimilarities to Forester's heroine, Hepburn was a good fifteen years older and therefore somewhat past the point of exploding with adolescent sexuality. But steamy passion had, even in her earliest years as an actress, never been Hepburn's stock-in-trade. What Hepburn lacked in voluptuousness, though, she made up for in wit; and in lightning-fast, highly verbal comedies, such as Howard Hawks's *Bringing Up Baby* (1938) and Cukor's *The Philadelphia Story* (1940), she was in her element. Huston must have known that if he did not steer *The African Queen* toward comedy, he would have wasted one of his heroine's greatest assets.

If there was an element of self-indulgence to Huston's forcing his cast and crew to endure the miseries of central Africa, a more positive side to that same headstrong independent streak was his ability not to feel constricted by his own reputation as a chronicler of tragic, doomed quests. Though he was not known as a director of comedy and his material did not ostensibly require it, Huston was flexible enough to exploit the opportunity anyway. The film's finest moments come when Bogart and Hepburn confront their gigantic differences. When she speaks of her nostalgia for the peaceful Sunday afternoon back in her beloved England, he responds bluntly that "on Sunday afternoons I was always sleeping one off." When he collapses in relief that they have not drowned or been dashed against the rocks after a particularly treacherous stretch of rapids, she observes blithely, "I never dreamed any mere physical sensation could be so stimulating." Then when Bogart seeks his own stimulation in the form of "a drop too much" of gin, excusing himself by pointing out that "it's only human nature," she archly explains that "nature, Mr. Allnutt, is what we are put into this world to rise above." After a hundred minutes of such repartee, interspersed with preposterously adventurous feats, Huston was then faced with either remaining consistent with his own reputation and, in doing so, loyal to Forester's book, or inventing an ending worthy of the silliness that preceded it. He opted for silliness.

Even before the story was fitted to the personalities of Hepburn and Bogart, however, its ending needed work. Forester himself was re-

portedly unhappy with it and tried a different version in the book's
American edition than he had used in the English. After all the tribulations Rose and Allnutt had endured in getting down the savage river,
Forester could not bring himself to let them perish. But their goal of
sinking a huge German cruiser was so farfetched that neither did he
feel they could credibly succeed. They thus do neither and the reader
is left unsatisfied, without a climax worthy of what has preceded. Huston, if he was to run true to form, should have arranged for the couple
to have met an ignoble end, succumbing to some weakness within
themselves after having so heroically triumphed over all exterior ob-
stacles. Perhaps had he found some ironic fate for his protagonists, his
critics would have found the film full of "depth and distinction." But
he took a more heretical approach: "I thought the film should have a
happy ending," he said (*OB*, 190).

What he contrived was an emotionally satisfying resolution that
matched the highly fanciful nature of the story perfectly. Even Forester agreed. With their boat sunk and themselves captured and about to
be hanged by the Germans they had wanted to attack, Hepburn and
Bogart were in a position not unlike that of Bogart surrounded by Japanese at the end of *Across the Pacific*. Yet this time it was not outlandish heroism that saved the day but a sublime instance of deus ex
machina: the submerged hull of the *African Queen*, fitted with the
torpedoes that were supposed to ram the German ship, is instead
rammed by its target, thus producing the same effect. The conclusion
in its comical way is a complementary one to that of *Sierra Madre*,
where a last-minute twist of fate had brought failure, and Walter Huston's philosophical response is equally applicable: "Laugh. It's a great
joke played on us by the Lord, fate, nature, or whatever you prefer,
but whoever, whatever, certainly had a sense of humor." Critics may
have agreed that the finale was, as one put it, "wildly melodramatic,"
but Huston had every right to insist that cosmic jokes did not always
have to be cruel. In doing so, he made a movie that was hugely popular, won himself Oscar nominations for both screenplay and direction,
and an Oscar for Bogart as the year's best actor, and lost the respect of
the highbrow critics.

It had been a year of extremes for Huston; 1951 had begun with a
series of disheartening previews of *The Red Badge of Courage*. The
previews had indicated that the strength of his study of cowardice and
courage was lost on most audiences, and those at the studio who had
first supported it were now against it. The project's critics at the studio
were now emboldened to meddle with his conception of the work.
Finally, the whole exasperating experience was to be preserved and
transmitted to the world in the form of a book that would accuse him
of professional irresponsibility.

But by the middle of the year Huston was thousands of miles away from Hollywood. In the African jungle his rule was undisputed. He could indulge his passion for adventure and his every order was carried out with no questions asked. The production was an independent one, and the only man who could possibly have exercised any authority over the director was his partner Sam Spiegel. Yet when Spiegel attempted to check up on things in Africa, Huston reportedly hired hundreds of chanting natives to impede his movements until the beleagured producer gave up and departed. Nor did Huston consider going back to California for the necessary studio work; that was taken care of in London where, by the standards of the depressed English film industry, *The African Queen*, with its Technicolor, big stars, and lavish production values, was accorded great respect.

Huston's career as a cog in the Hollywood production machine was over. His success at plying his trade far away from studio supervision was partly a function of his wanderlust, adventurous spirit, and disinclination to be fenced in; but it was also a result of the eroded power of the studio system itself. Gravely weakened by the competition of television, the results of antitrust litigation, and the passing of the old generation of industry moguls, the studios could no longer control their employees as they had in previous decades. Huston's timing had proved providential. Just as he had been lucky to have been given *The Maltese Falcon* as his first assignment, and lucky to have escaped being killed in the Aleutians or in Italy during the war, he was lucky to have had the benefit of the solid training of traditional Hollywood and then have the ironclad rules that governed the old system conveniently break down just as he was scoring his biggest box office success. As 1952 began, Huston was in an enviable position. He had learned his trade in the most sophisticated moviemaking center in the world; then, just as it was showing signs of decline, he shook himself free of it by proving he could make profitable films elsewhere.

In his wheeling and dealing to finance *The African Queen*, Sam Spiegel had arranged with Romulus Films, a London production company headed by two brothers, John and James Woolf, to exchange, for funds advanced, European distribution rights to the film. Back from Africa, Huston had wearied of dealing with Spiegel, but he got on well with the Woolf brothers and with them he planned his next film. James Woolf had suggested to Huston that he consider filming a fictionalized account of the life of the painter Henri de Toulouse-Lautrec by Pierre La Mure. A French writer who had been the American correspondent for various European newspapers, La Mure settled permanently in America during World War II and began writing in English. He had written a version of the life of the famous postimpressionist painter that was stronger on contrived romance than on the often unsavory truth about Lautrec's life. This, his first novel published in his second language, became Huston's tenth feature.

Moulin Rouge (1952)

The idea of seeking an equivalent in cinematic terms for the visual effect of Toulouse-Lautrec's painting seems to have been Huston's motivating interest in the project. Whether or not he had actually spent a year as a starving artist in Paris two decades earlier, Huston had a genuine interest in painting. He had dabbled in it as a hobby and invested in it as a collector. And now, just at the point in his career when he was the freest to do anything he wanted, he chose the world of painting as the subject of a film.

Surely Huston was not drawn to the life of Toulouse-Lautrec because of its sensational nature. The film he made proves that he was so exclusively interested in visual ideas that he was willing to neglect dramatic ones. The choice of La Mure's sanitized version of the painter's life was in itself a deliberate abstention from biographical or historical concerns. Interviewed twenty-five years later, Huston was frank in acknowledging as much: "There was a sentimental turn to the film that, if anything, would have offended the painter himself who was clinically detached. . . . I felt even at the time it's a shame we can't make the true story of Lautrec. We had to understand and accept what we could and could not show. Not only instinctively, it was laid down in the Code. We went as far as we could. When I contemplate the censorship at that time and the absurdities of it, it is hard to believe."[4]

What Huston was referring to was Toulouse-Lautrec's penchant for brothel life. The subject of prostitution was not among those permitted by the Production Code. Its existence could occasionally be hinted at as a fate worse than death for "bad" women, but portraying it as a background for daily life, as it was for Toulouse-Lautrec, was out of the question. The fact that, during the period of his life that Huston sought to deal with, Toulouse-Lautrec virtually resided in brothels and was treated as a family member by the women who worked there completely precluded any honest treatment of his life. That and little else would account for Huston's using La Mure's pseudobiographical novel rather than more factual sources as the basis for his story.

The choice of an actor to play the artist was not one Huston could have made even if he wanted to. Jose Ferrer already owned the rights to La Mure's book and intended to adapt it to the stage with himself in the lead role. Huston apparently welcomed the idea of starring him in the film, but it is uncertain whether he could have acquired the property in the first place if he had refused to use Ferrer. In any case, both men benefited: Huston got an actor who handled the role well, and Ferrer got his material put to far better use than would ever have been possible on the stage. For without its cinematographic effects, the material would not have amounted to much.

La Mure's story sterilized the circumstances of Toulouse-Lautrec's life and then dressed it up with some conventional love interest. Even after Huston collaborated with his "favorite American screenwriter," Anthony Veiller (with whom he had worked right after the war on the scripts for *The Stranger* and *The Killers*), the narrative was not a compelling one. It largely contented itself with a glum recounting of two failed love affairs, one with a prostitute (referred to in the press of the day variously as a "street girl," a "witch of the streets," and a "vixen of the streets") played by French actress Colette Marchand, and another with a fashion model, also played by a Frenchwoman unknown on the American screen, Suzanne Flon. Throughout the film's almost two hours, Ferrer spends most of the time drinking and making acerbic reflections on his lot in life: "Some men can swing by their heels from a flying trapeze, some can become president of the republic. *I* can drink cognac." Or, to his unfaithful lover, "It's not our ideas that bind us together, it's failure. . . . The streets of Paris have taught you to strike quickly and draw blood. . . . I am a painter of the streets and of the gutter." The artist's work, according to the film, is held in blatant contempt; his own father snarls, "Work? It's a pretext to hang around cheap dance halls and drink all night. You call that pornographic trash work?" Dramatically, especially compared to the richness of incident and variety of tempo in all of Huston's previous work, *Moulin Rouge* is a one-note film.

The director's attention was elsewhere. And that elsewhere was the attempt to bend the Technicolor process to his personal ends. Previously when working from literary sources he admired, Huston had demonstrated an extraordinary fidelity to their author's vision. Given the complexity of moving from a verbal medium to a visual one, his ability to do so was most impressive. With *Moulin Rouge*, Huston embarked on a similar effort except that his source was already in a visual medium. His loyalty this time was not to a book but to its subject. And since the true story of its subject could not, because of the Production Code, be brought to the screen, Huston was left with Toulouse-Lautrec's art.

His aim was not to record an art director's version of famous artists' work (as Vincente Minnelli had just done in 1951 in his musical *An American in Paris*), but to evoke the painter's vision using the camera itself. The idea was an unconventional one and to help with it the director went to a still photographer known for his experiments with color, Eliot Elisofon. The two had met in Africa during the shooting of *The African Queen*, and the director had been intrigued by the pho-

tographer's ideas. "Since movies are a form of fiction," Elisofon was to
say later in an interview, "how much better to make the color fictional
too! I never believed that color in pictures ought to be a facsimile of
the real thing. Good artists take what they like from reality and discard
the rest. Back in the Renaissance, painters were already using certain
glazes of transparent color to get an effect of luminosity. I hold that
filters are to a photographer what glazes are to a painter."[5] Elisofon,
after a close study of Toulouse-Lautrec's painting and some still photographic tests on the streets of Paris, worked closely with *Moulin
Rouge*'s cinematographer, Oswald Morris, to put his theories to work.
Logical as they seemed however, his ideas were anathema to the Technicolor company who, though responsible for processing and printing
the film, disclaimed all responsibility for the results.

Huston deserves no small thanks for promoting the idea that color
cinematography need not be a postcardlike mimicry of so-called natural color. Eventually misty, almost monochromatic color would become
a style almost as common as its opposite. So those qualities in *Moulin
Rouge* need to be recognized for their originality to be fully appreci-
ated. If the traditional advantage of photography over painting at first
was that it was closer to "reality," the same was later said of the difference between photography in black and white and that in color. It took
photographers a while to realize that their medium was no less subjective than painting, and the realization was just as slow in coming in
regard to color photography as it had been with black and white. The
conventional wisdom, upheld by the Technicolor laboratory, was that
the duty of color cinematography was to be more "lifelike" than black
and white. Huston realized how groundless this concept was and that
nothing was stopping him from using the Technicolor process to choose
what he wanted from reality.

Moulin Rouge is less a dramatic narrative than a splendid evocation
of opulent cabarets, the rosy gas-lit inferno of raucous dance-halls,
flowing dresses tossed about in uninhibited dancing, cold aquamarine
facades along deserted Paris streets at night, the glow of silverware in
elegant restaurants, the pale yellow light of dawn over the Seine, the
dusky flanks of thoroughbreds on verdant racecourses. The images may
not be literal transcriptions of Lautrec's canvases but they have a se-
ductive allure of their own. And there are a couple of sequences that
focus directly and powerfully on Lautrec's art itself. One offers a de-
tailed view of the technical processes of lithography, culminating in the
pulling of richly colored posters off huge presses. Another abandons
all connection to the story and presents a pure montage of Toulouse-
Lautrec's images carefully edited to the music of the dance halls in
which he found so many of his subjects. The sequence is particularly
satisfying in that it seems to realize the film's repressed ambition: to

revel in the pure visual poetry of Toulouse-Lautrec's art without regard to narrative. Ultimately a two-hour narrative film with a weak narrative, *Moulin Rouge* must be judged a failure. But after the easy, conventional success of *The African Queen*, there remains something admirable in Huston's appetite for this difficult, unorthodox project.

Though an artistic gamble, *Moulin Rouge* turned out not to have been a commercial one. Huston's name, the success of *The African Queen*, the glamour that surrounded Toulouse-Lautrec, the world of art, and the "gay nineties" in Paris, all worked in the film's behalf. If the moviegoing public were let down by the production's dramatic deficiencies, it was only after enough of them had purchased tickets to insure its profitability. If Huston had had any misgivings about cutting his ties with Hollywood and operating in Europe on his own, two consecutive successful films were surely enough to dissolve them. From Paris, he moved his family to County Kildare, Ireland, bought a grand manor house, and took up life as a country gentleman. Huston loved the people and landscape of Ireland; the low cost of living and freedom from American taxes were also appealing for they enabled him to live like a lord. Perhaps it was the sensation that he was sitting on top of the world that encouraged him to permit himself the most cockeyed, spontaneous, and unpredictable movie he ever directed.

Beat the Devil (1954)

A novel had come to his attention written by James Helvick, a pseudonym for a journalist named Claude Cockburn. The author's goal had been modest: he needed money to support his life as a member of Ireland's landed gentry and hoped his quickly written potboiler would earn him some. The story was about a group of criminals and a swindling scheme involving uranium. Though there were elements reminiscent of *The Maltese Falcon*—eccentric crooks and an exotic quest—Huston surely knew that Helvick was no Hammett and the book no literary classic. His motives in pursuing its adaptation to the screen were more likely goodwill toward an Irish neighbor and just the hunch that working on it might be fun.

Never one to have capital available for anything besides horses and good living, Huston could not begin to finance the project, but he prevailed upon his colleague Humphrey Bogart to do so. Back in comfortable Hollywood after the rigors of Africa, Bogart, who had always managed his salary better than did his favorite director, agreed to buy the rights to the book and put up money to develop a script. His backing plus that of the Woolf brothers got *Beat the Devil* off the ground.

Huston's next steps were perfectly consistent with his normal working methods: he contacted his now perennial collaborator Anthony

Veiller as well as *African Queen* contributor Peter Viertel (whose vili-
fication of the director in his novel about the experience, *White Hunter, Black Heart,* apparently had not dampened their friendship) and
enlisted their help in the preparation of a script. Arrangements were
made to shoot on location in Ravello, a beautiful village on the Italian
coast south of Naples. Joining Bogart in the cast were Jennifer Jones,
veteran of *We Were Strangers,* and, stirring up echoes of *The Maltese
Falcon,* Peter Lorre. A kind of Sydney Greenstreet surrogate was
found in Robert Morley, whose brief role in *The African Queen* had
provided some of that film's best moments. Added sex appeal was contributed by Italian screen goddess Gina Lollobrigida. With a script in
hand and a crew that included *Moulin Rouge* cinematographer Oswald
Morris assembled in an idyllic setting, all seemed set for well-orga-
nized moviemaking. There was, however, one unresolved problem:
the script.

"It just didn't pan out," said Huston, "I was pretty discouraged about
our chances of getting any kind of picture, and I proposed that we
abandon the whole thing."[6] It was a situation that would occur often in
his career, but not often with as happy an ending. Into the fray jumped
Truman Capote. The diminutive, foppish writer ("epicene," Huston
called him) was as remote a figure from the hard-boiled virile style of
Bogart and Huston as could possibly have been imagined. But he had
two invaluable qualities to offer the imperiled project: writing talent
and proximity. Capote was living in Rome and agreed to come down
to Ravello to see what he could do with the ailing script. His job was
not simply one of polishing basically solid material (such as Viertel had
done with Agee's work on *The African Queen*), but to start all over
again and try to find a way to produce a usable script where Veiller
and Viertel could not. As if this was not already an ambitious enough
goal, Capote had to work without the luxury of time. Each day's installment was written as the previous one's was being shot. Huston at
first managed to invent delays to give Capote a head start but the
shooting always threatened to catch up with his writing. It was not a
serious way to write a script and there was absolutely nothing serious
about the result.

Huston himself later described the tactics he and Capote were reduced to: "because I didn't want the company to know how bankrupt
we were in so far as pages were concerned, I staged an elaborate scene
that would take some time to prepare. They had to knock out a wall,
and it was very difficult, the way I staged the scene. Then I went
upstairs and joined Truman and we did our writing. We were able to
work for two hours and write another scene—the one we shot."[7] Despite the fact that every such chaotic day was costing thousands of dollars, Huston seemed unperturbed. If he suspected that his

improvisatory efforts to keep the script ahead of shooting might at any time falter and bring the whole affair to an expensive dead end, he did not let such misgivings dampen his spirits.

If anyone had reason to be anxious, it was Bogart, who had more than half a million dollars of his own money invested in the production, but he was apparently taken in by Huston's air of self-assurance and, though reportedly mystified about the exact nature of the character he was playing, did his best to follow his director's instructions. Huston had shown Bogart how to play Sam Spade and Charlie Allnutt, and he now told him how to play a most peculiar American businessman named Billy Dannreuther. "Bogey was always ever so obedient," Huston recalled. "He would try to get what I wanted. He wasn't really against the film as we were making it."[8] Nor did the other actors, all collecting hefty salaries, have any reason to question Huston's purposes. Jennifer Jones, in a blond wig, bubbled with schoolgirl charm. Gina Lollobrigida was too busy struggling with the phonetics of the English language to worry about what her lines meant, and Peter Lorre acted as if he were far beyond troubling himself about what, if anything, the whole thing might be about. Only Robert Morley appeared incredulous at the rampant absurdity that surrounded him. For that very reason his character dominates the film: he alone seems to share the audience's bewilderment.

Not only did *Beat the Devil* never bother to declare its true colors to its audience, it seemed never to have revealed them—Morley possibly excepted—to its own cast. Huston and Capote, in their feverish last-minute scripting, drifted further and further into a gigantic private joke. Perhaps Huston thought that Bogart would have rebelled if he suspected the extent of the frivolity, and, in fact, the actor was outraged when he saw the result. But ultimately, the work's appeal lies in its deviousness.

The deviousness begins just minutes into the film when after the introduction of the story's main characters—described by Bogart's narration as "brilliant criminals"—Jennifer Jones remarks that "they're desperate characters—not one of them looked at my legs!" Random bits of philosophy are soon offered up with only the flimsiest of motivation. Lorre ponders the true nature of time, observing that "the Swiss manufacture it, the Italians squander it, and the Americans say it's money." Should the viewer be uncertain how to react, the rotund Morley helpfully explains that "a good laugh does more for the stomach muscles than five minutes' sitting-up exercises." Soon, as the intrigue about crooked uranium dealing plods listlessly on, absurdity begins to take control. Jones, in the most unmistakably nasal of middle American accents, presents herself as a blue-blooded Englishwoman and remarks, when meeting Bogart, "I've never talked to an American before." He in turn introduces himself: "I'm a typical rare spirit, I was an orphan until I was twenty, then a rich and beautiful woman adopted me." Jones, never at a loss for words, replies: "You're going to Africa to become a king and you need a beautiful blonde queen." (An African queen?, one wonders.) The setting behind her as she throws herself into Bogart's arms, precipitous cliffs dropping off to a secluded beach hundreds of feet below, somehow matches the capricious nature of the dialogue.

The confusion of nationalities was an inevitable by-product of Huston's increasingly international brand of filmmaking. Beginning with *The African Queen,* one of the few, perhaps the only, consistent element in Huston's work was its refusal to stay within the boundaries of a single nation. The financing of a film might come from one country, its cast and crew from a variety of others, its exteriors filmed in a nation far removed from the one that provided the studio for its interiors. If these were nominally considered American films, it could only have been because their director was American. And eventually even that fact was to be muddied by Huston's adopting Irish citizenship. It was thus quite fitting that one of the central motifs of *Beat the Devil's* humor should be the mixing-up of nationality.

Here was a novel written by an Englishman living in Ireland, turned into a movie script by four Americans, one living in Venice (Veiller), another in Switzerland (Viertel), another in Rome (Capote), and the last in Ireland (Huston). Money came from London and Hollywood. The cinematographer was British, the cast variously American (Bogart, Jones), British (Morley), and Italian (Lollobrigida). And then there was Peter Lorre, an actor who was born in Hungary and worked in Austria and Switzerland before gaining fame in Germany and then fleeing to America. The production's location was, of course, Italy. In the film, Lorre (dressed up to look like the American Capote) presents himself as a German from Chile; "It drinks, it smokes, it philosophizes!" exclaims an amazed Bogart upon meeting him. Jones explains English life to the ever-incredulous Morley and quotes from the wise sayings of her "old Spanish nurse" such as "half the people on earth would be ruined at once if everyone told what they knew." No more than three minutes later she refers to her as her "old French nurse." Bogart's character is an American living in Italy with his Italian wife (Lollobrigida), whose spirit, he says, is English. The whole diverse crew is off to Africa where, if they can escape from the Arab sheik who captures them, it is their intention to sell vacuum cleaners "hut-to-hut." They are all true to Jones's expressed philosophy that "nowadays one simply can't afford to dismiss people simply because they are not one's sort."

There were two main reactions to the final result of the nonsensical project. Huston himself admitted that "you can't get more trivial" and stated simply that it was "made in the spirit of fun, and it was a hell of a lark doing it." Critics on the whole seemed to accept the film in the spirit that Huston proposed, and called it "a kind of shell game with the operator sometimes forgetting under which shell the black ball is hidden" and "as elaborate a shaggy-dog story as has ever been told." Bogart, however, did not agree and was quoted as saying that "only the phonies think it's funny—it's a mess."[10] His bitterness stemmed surely from the fact that the joke had been, literally, at his expense. Audiences were not at first responsive and Bogart lost the money he had so confidently invested in Huston's talent. Sadly, the actor was not to survive to see *Beat the Devil* grow in popularity and be recognized for the screwball masterwork that it is.

7

Rough Waters and Calm

Moby Dick (1956)

"THERE ARE CERTAIN queer times and occasions in this strange mixed affair we call life when a man takes this whole universe for a vast practical joke, though the wit thereof he but dimly discerns, and more than suspects that the joke is at nobody's expense but his own. . . . And as for small difficulties and worryings, prospects of sudden disaster, peril of life and limb; all these and death itself, seem to him only sly, good-natured hits, and jolly punches in the side bestowed by the unseen and unaccountable old joker."[1]

The writer of the above lines was not working on a script for a film starring Walter Huston and directed by his son. Herman Melville had written *Moby Dick* over a century earlier. But bringing the novel to the screen seemed in many ways a task preordained for John Huston. It has often been called the greatest work of American literature, and Huston had built his reputation on adapting literature skillfully to the screen. It was a story about men in dangerous circumstances, just as Huston's war documentaries, *Sierra Madre*, *The Asphalt Jungle*, and *The Red Badge of Courage* had been; and it recounted the adventures of a heterogeneous band of characters engaged in a doomed quest, just as had almost every film Huston had directed. *Moby Dick* was to be a pivotal film for Huston.

It was partly an accident of circumstance that the project came at such a critical juncture in Huston's career, for he had had an adaptation of the novel in mind since the early forties when he had wanted his father in the central role of the demented Captain Ahab. And Walter Huston might well have been more powerful in the part than the actor who did play it, Gregory Peck. The critical consensus on what Huston was to call "the most difficult picture I've ever done" was that, because of Peck's inadequacy, it was hollow at its center. But if Huston had shot *Moby Dick* before his father's death, he would have done it at a time when he was under strict studio supervision and not a freewheeling

Gregory Peck as Captain Ahab impaled on the white whale in Moby Dick. Courtesy of the Museum of Modern Art, Film Stills Archive.

77

international celebrity, able to marshal the resources of many nations to his personal ends.

In fact, the practically unanimous verdict by the critics that the film failed because of Peck's unsuitability ("a peg-legged Abe Lincoln," complained *Time*)[2] must have been particularly galling to the director, because casting Peck had been such a minor concern compared to the gigantic ones of reconstructing a nineteenth-century whaling voyage on the high seas. Huston's position was in ironic contrast to the two earlier attempts to exploit Melville's novel on the screen. Both earlier films had been made for Warner Brothers (who were also backing Huston's venture), and both had sported the bombastic John Barrymore in the Ahab role. The first version was silent; even with its title changed to *The Sea Beast* (1926), it could not escape disparaging comparisons with its source, reviewers pointing out that its story was "garbled beyond decency." The second movie *Moby Dick* (1930) kept the novel's title but "improved" its story with some love interest in the person of Joan Bennett, playing Ahab's sweetheart. As an early "talkie," there was no question of its action straying far from the cumbersome microphones on the Warners soundstage. Again the great white whale was, as in the first film, in a reviewer's words, "a particularly lifeless example of poor studio machinery, as ferocious and menacing as a ferry boat."[3] Curiously, it was the feeble special effects, not the disparity between Barrymore's histrionics and Melville's complex vision of a man at war with God, that were mainly remarked upon.

Inappropriate as it may have been though, Barrymore's Ahab seemed to have unconsciously remained the definitive one in the minds of critics. "How Barrymore could have played Ahab for Huston!" one of them lamented.[4] Defending Peck years later, Huston argued that "what many people had seen in the original Barrymore version of *Moby Dick* had led them to expect an Ahab of wild gestures and staring eyes: that wasn't Melville" (*OB*, 258).

Since Huston, whatever his failings, cannot be accused of insensitivity to his actors and since his defense cannot be considered promotional hyperbole, coming so long after the film's commercial fate (a less than happy one) had been decided, his opinion deserves consideration. Reviewers perhaps had difficulties shedding memories of the more benign roles Peck had recently played—that of the earnest crusader against anti-Semitism in Elia Kazan's *Gentlemen's Agreement* (1947), or that of the carefree American reporter in William Wyler's *Roman Holiday* (1953)—but that was neither the fault of Peck nor of Huston. Another obvious problem was one that neither John Barrymore nor Walter Huston nor anyone else could have surmounted: the fact that

Melville's Ahab was more than a peculiar individual sea captain. He was an icon for all mankind's blind, obsessional rage against its own impotence and insignificance. No mere beard or whale-bone peg leg could turn an actor into the embodiment of all the metaphorical weight that Melville had invested in Ahab. Nor could the author's physical descriptions have been of much help to movie makeup artists: "He looked like a man cut away from the stake, when the fire has overrunningly wasted all the limbs without consuming them, or taking away one particle from their compact aged robustness." This time there was little opportunity for the kind of happy marriage between an author's vision and an actor's gifts that had turned Bogart into Hammett's Sam Spade.

Despite the grumblings about what, from the perspective of several decades, seems a very honorable attempt on Peck's part to portray Ahab, not a single critic at the time ventured any complaint about Huston's overall interpretation of Melville's novel. The dense and convoluted prose, the long digressive discussions on the history, mythology, and technical details of the whaling industry, the often abstruse maritime jargon ("But Ahab is lord over the level load-stone yet, Mr. Starbuck—a lance without a pole; a top-maul, and the smallest of the sail-maker's needles."), made absolute fidelity to the novel an almost impossible task. Although there is, of necessity, a greater than usual distance between Huston and his literary source, even his severest critics did not accuse him of disloyalty to the spirit of Melville's book. When compared to the two Barrymore versions, Huston's respect for his source seems positively devout.

The adaptation began with Huston's selection of Ray Bradbury, a writer of science fiction with no previous movie experience, to prepare a script. Bradbury's task was an intimidating one; he had to weave the discursive richness of the book into sequences of pure action, transfer the silent ruminations of its characters into spoken dialogue, and rearrange its dramatic incidents to accomodate a pared-down cast of characters. "It was exhausting," he later admitted, "I read the book at least nine times, and rewrote some of the scenes up to thirty times. In all, I did 1,500 pages to get a final 150. . . . I found myself plagued with a vast depression. I felt I had the weight, the burden of Melville on my back."[5] Squeezed between his responsibility to the great author and the domineering personality of his director, Bradbury had little good will left for the latter by the time he had finished. He objected bitterly to Huston's sharing credit for the script, appealing to the arbitration of the Screen Writers' Guild to order Huston's name removed as coscenarist. The justice of Bradbury's claim could only be established by an eyewitness to the hours he spent writing at Huston's Irish home. But given the director's experience as a screenwriter himself and his physical presence during both the scripting and the shooting (when last-minute dialogue changes would not have been unusual), Bradbury's case seemed more a symptom of nervous exhaustion than a clear-cut issue of authorship. The Screen Writers' Guild backed Huston.

Even if it were to be decisively proved that not a word of *Moby Dick*'s dialogue could be traced to its director, however, it would no less demand to be considered as the work of John Huston. The principal source of the film's impact is not in its script. Once again Huston and cinematographer Oswald Morris were to discard the conventional realism of the Technicolor process in favor of a stylized look they considered more appropriate to their material. The stylization was of an entirely different nature than that of *Moulin Rouge*, however. Where that film had been suffused with color, *Moby Dick* was to be selectively drained of it; instead of a tone inspired by Toulouse-Lautrec's vibrantly colored lithographs, they wanted the quality of somber old engravings of seafaring life. Experimentation started, as it had in Paris, with still photographs taken at prospective locations that were then manipulated in the laboratory to find a way to mute the colors to suggest, as Morris said, "that this story was filmed in 1843 when it was supposed to have taken place."[6] The laboratory side of the work proved relatively simple: two sets of negative film were prepared, one in black and white, the other in standard Technicolor. Prints were then struck by combining both negatives so that the black and white muted the color in a way that seemed to give it a patina of age. The process, though, was equally dependent on careful judgment about the actual filming conditions—conditions that were far harder to control than negatives in a laboratory.

Bright, sunny days were avoided; dull, leaden skies, and cold rain were preferred. The stretch of Irish seacoast Huston had selected for the re-creation of old New Bedford was frequently blessed with such gloomy conditions. For shooting at sea, turbulent waters suited the color scheme better than tranquil ones. And so a century-old three-masted schooner refitted as a New Bedford whaler, several mechanical whales, and a large cast and crew were repeatedly put in the most dangerous of circumstances. The film's drama could perhaps have been brought to life in safer quarters, but Huston and Morris were apparently convinced that the visual quality that they sought for it could not.

"It was one of the stormiest seasons in the history of those seas," Huston recalled as he described the shooting off the coast of Wales and Portugal. "Lifeboats were capsized. I don't mean our boats, but the coastal lifeboats that went out to vessels in distress. Ships were blown on the rocks. We were dismasted three times. Once there was no question in my mind we were heading for the bottom and were just saved by a miracle of seamanship."[7] Tales of lives risked, props destroyed, and cast members injured were, of course, standard grist for the publicity mill of any adventure movie. And Huston had always recounted them with relish even when, as was the case with *The African Queen*, they had little to do with what was on the screen. But this was not the case with *Moby Dick;* perils faced during its production were not irrelevant. It may seem ingenuous that Huston wrote in his autobiography that "the picture, like the book, is a blasphemy, so I suppose we can just lay it to God's defending Himself when He sent those awful winds and waves against us" (*OB*, 251). The visual effect of the film indicates that Huston was not being flippant.

The idea of blasphemy first takes a verbal form in a flamboyant cameo performance by Orson Welles as Melville's fire-and-brimstone preacher who "had been a sailor and harpooner in his youth, but for many years past had dedicated his life to the ministry." Welles, reportedly without the benefit of rehearsals but not without that of brandy, holds forth on the perils of defying God's will with obvious relish. Welles bellows so thunderously that he seems in danger of sliding into self-caricature in the manner of *Beat the Devil's* Robert Morley. But before he can, Huston strikes a serious note. With Welles's words still resounding, there follows a moving sequence of the whaler Pequod putting out to sea, the sad faces of the town's womenfolk lining the dock, and the chanty-singing crew scrambling about the ship's rigging. Morris's camera is mounted high atop the mast giving an acrophobic view of the busy deck below; then another shot from water level looks up at the majestic bow plowing forward and the billowing sails above it. Then a wistful long shot of the town shrinking on the horizon is partly masked by those sails while the whole frame is bathed in a warm sepia light and a sunset glow bounces off the sea.

The simultaneous majesty and dread of a whaling voyage is captured from the beginning, and the stage set splendidly for "our supreme lord and dictator," as the narrator, Ishmael—ably played by Richard Basehart—calls him, who "stayed behind locked doors all the daylight hours." The demented Ahab seems truly satanic as he is first heard— his "barbaric white leg," made from whale bone, pounding rhythmically against the wooden deck during his nocturnal pacings—and then seen. Peck's grizzled visage is marked by the long scar that Melville had described as "a slender rod-like mark, lividly whitish" which "resembled that perpendicular seam sometimes made in the straight, lofty trunk of a great tree, when the lightning tearingly darts down it, and without wrenching a single twig, peels and grooves out the bark from top to bottom, ere running off into the soil, leaving the tree still green- ly alive but branded." Again the prow of the great ship is seen cutting through the waves just after Ahab has bellowed his venomous threat, "God strike us all if we do not hunt Moby Dick to his death."

The process of attacking and killing whales was on so grandiose a scale that it was little wonder the attempts to portray it inside a studio in the Barrymore versions of the story seemed ridiculous. Nor was it surprising that the hunting scenes gave Huston the most trouble. Working in turbulent seas with ninety-foot-long models of whales— the first two of which sank during storms—was a task requiring both sophisticated engineering and foolhardy risk taking. The result was bound to have been impressive in a purely mechanical sense, but the film's whaling sequences overwhelm in a way that precludes any notice being taken of the technique behind it. With the camera in the position of an oarsman in one of the harpooner's boats, waves splash over the lens as the men approach their prey. Under dark, menacing skies, a whale's giant tail dwarfs the fragile-looking boats, his spouting can be glimpsed through the surf beating against the camera lens. Then comes the hurling of the harpoon and the huge beast is spouting blood. A few minutes later there are vertiginous shots, from a camera mount- ed high in the rigging, of the rolling ship and then a view through a telescope as Ishmael spots a school of hundreds of whales on the ho- rizon. Then the camera is again tossed about on board the fragile craft racing to the kill, catching the flight of the harpoons and then the sea going red with spilled blood. One of the leviathans opens and closes his jaws in anguish before rolling over dead. The spectacle is extraor- dinary for its vividness. Whatever contrivances and machinations were employed to create such images, the viewer is not aware of them. *Moby Dick's* whaling sequences are high achievements of action filmmaking.

The climactic scene wherein the man who would "strike the sun if it insulted me" is humbled by the monstrous forces he presumed to challenge departs a bit from Melville, but brilliantly so. Instead of dis- apearing into the sea, caught by the rope of a harpoon imbedded in Moby Dick as he churns away, Ahab is lashed to his prey, drowned, and brought to the surface again. The limp motion of his lifeless arm seems to beckon others to join him in his watery grave. It was a Huston touch of which Melville would certainly have approved and a fitting finish to a film that, if one ever could, does justice to the greatest of American novels.

Over fifteen years and as many films, John Huston had fought with intelligence and integrity to do the best work he could in an industry where neither virtue always prevailed. He had gained acclaim with his very first film and, despite commercial ups and downs, had largely held onto critical and popular favor. More important, no film to which he had signed his name had ever been ploddingly conventional; his failures had always been more interesting than many directors' successes. Now he had fought his hardest war to date and emerged with a movie that was striking to look at, full of rousing action, and worthy of the literary landmark from which it had been drawn. To *Moby Dick* there could be no sequel and his next project was far removed from its predecessor. It was as simple as *Moby Dick* had been complex, drawn from a novel as banal as Melville's was inspired, and shot in a locale as benign as the North Atlantic had been brutal. That Huston had sought solace from the rigors of *Moby Dick* was not surprising; the result is as good, maybe even a better film.

Heaven Knows, Mr. Allison (1957)

The contrast between the two projects distinctly recalls that between *The Red Badge of Courage* and *The African Queen*. In both cases, Huston moved from large-scale, all-male spectacle based on a literary classic to an intimate study of the relationship between a man and a woman cut off from the rest of the world, drawn from a source unimposing enough to leave him free to alter it to suit himself. In both cases he left behind logistical problems of military proportions to create a satisfying drama out of the simplest of ingredients. On the surface, even the characters seemed the same: an ill-bred ruffian whom circumstances toss into an isolated situation with a prim and pious maiden. *The African Queen* had been primarily a comedy and had been shot under rugged conditions, whereas *Heaven Knows, Mr. Allison* was more subdued in tone and shot in a more commodious locale; but both proved a therapeutic change of pace from big productions that seemed to bring out the best in the director.

Some things, of course, had changed. Huston, though still independent by the standards of the old studio system, was not this time working for a maverick producer like Sam Spiegel but for 20th Century-Fox, with which he had just signed a three-film contract. The high-living director needed a way to pay his mounting debts and, when *Moby Dick* proved less than a smashing success at the box office, it was imperative that he keep working whether the material offered him seemed agreeable or not. In the case of an unexceptional novel based on the salacious possibilities of a rough-hewn marine and an angelic nun marooned together on a tropical island, the material must have seemed downright disagreeable. Contrarily, with *The African Queen*, Huston had been fond of the Forester novel and had hand-picked his scenarist, James Agee. This time he disliked his source ("a very bad novel," he called it, which he had already "rejected as a possibility for a film" [*OB*, 260]) and had no say in who adapted it, since it had already been assigned to a member of the resident Hollywood writing corps, John Lee Mahin.

Adding to the impression that Huston was being saddled with second-class material was a script from the same material that had already been discarded by William Wyler. The marine-nun non-love-affair tale then landed in Huston's none-too-willing lap. Instead of a bogus nun (as in the version offered Wyler), the veteran screenwriter decided that some ambiguity might be allowed in the relationship if she was genuine but had not yet taken her final vows, thus leaving the door to earthly temptation slightly ajar. The material was still far from what would seem the natural terrain of Huston, but if he still disliked it, he swallowed his distaste and dutifully went to work with Mahin. In five or six weeks working in Mexico (where Huston had retreated to celebrate his fiftieth birthday and recuperate from the shooting of *Moby Dick*), the two men finished a script with which the director professed satisfaction. With only two real speaking roles in the entire script (there was some talk between Japanese soldiers, but not in English), the project's fate rested on who would be hired to fill them.

The signing of Robert Mitchum and Deborah Kerr to the lead roles turned *Heaven Knows, Mr. Allison* from what might have been a work of dreary expediency for Huston into one of his most engaging films. The choice was a natural one on the part of the Fox authorities who negotiated it. Mitchum's career had been established by his portrayal of the quintessential American fighting man in William Wellman's *The Story of GI Joe* (1945) and though his range as an actor was wider than he usually had the chance to demonstrate, the role of a tough-talking marine was perfectly in keeping with his established screen image. British actress Deborah Kerr had been working in America for almost a decade, but it was an English film made just before her departure for Hollywood that most obviously recommended her for the role of the spirited Irish nun. In *Black Narcissus* (1947), directed by the team of Michael Powell and Emeric Pressburger, she had been memorable as the sister superior of a mission convent in the Himalayas who must set an example in the resistance of earthly temptations. The film had created controversy when released in America because of church objections to sequences depicting Kerr's life before becoming a nun. These scenes never reached American screens even though they were important to the story. Still, Fox's producers must have felt that the publicity the censorship had stirred would create some excitement about Kerr again playing a nun. Yet whatever imagination or lack of it was behind the pairing of Mitchum and Kerr, it turned out, in Huston's hands, to be a perfect one.

The single element in the planning of *Heaven Knows, Mr. Allison* that seemed to reflect the particular wishes of its director was its locale. However willing Huston was to take on a project assigned to him by a Hollywood studio, he was not about to go so far as to actually work in one. He arranged to shoot the film entirely on the tiny Caribbean island of Tobago, a British colony off the coast of Trinidad. "I picked Tobago for two reasons," Huston told an interviewer at the time. "I needed a place that was a dead ringer for a South Seas island, but I needed it nearer. And it had to be a spot where I could spend pounds sterling."[8] The second reason has a certain logic: British law made it difficult for American film companies to get the money they made in England converted into dollars so they found ways to channel their pounds back into productions. Though hardly a necessity, letting Huston work in a British colony had minor financial advantages for Fox. But Huston's first reason is harder to take seriously. Locations could surely have been found within a few minutes of the studio's offices, but most likely Huston just wanted the pleasures of a tropical resort far from the meddling hands of a studio. Installed on a lush Caribbean island with a script he had worked over to his satisfaction, Huston was in a promising position and he was to fulfill that promise stunningly.

The film opens majestically with shots of a lonely lifeboat adrift on the open seas as if the story of Ishmael, the lone survivor of *Moby Dick* were being continued. But a title soon informs the viewer that it is a century later and the scene is "somewhere in the South Pacific" in 1944, a year when dominion over that part of the globe was being savagely disputed by America and Japan. On the drifting craft lies a haggard Robert Mitchum. As he disembarks and wades ashore onto a paradisiacal beach, the camera tracks with him. Only the sound of the island's birds is on the soundtrack. The shipwrecked sailor, unsure of whether the island is in enemy hands, is cautious. He sees a small church, walks up to it, and meets its solitary occupant, a nun. After an unsettlingly mute opening sequence, the first words of the film are finally spoken. They are not just a natural beginning to the story but an accurate description of the whole tone of the film, Huston's plea for a deserved respite from the noisy extravaganza of *Moby Dick*. Says Robert Mitchum to Deborah Kerr: "Let's just keep it quiet, ma'am."

There follows a record, presented in a leisurely, matter-of-fact manner, of the tentative steps toward friendship between two very different human beings. Any sexual innuendo that might have seemed implicit in the situation is nowhere to be found. The two performers are both immensely appealing and totally credible. In between their uncertain attempts to get to know each other, there are exciting passages of action, notably a rousing underwater sequence of Mitchum attempting to capture a giant sea turtle for food. The island comes

Robert Mitchum plays a stranger in paradise. Courtesy of the Museum of Modern Art, Film Stills Archive.

under bombardment by American guns as Japanese forces storm ashore and a close-up of Kerr's terror-stricken face shakes as if, as in *San Pietro*, the cameraman himself had been jolted by the blasts. As the pair wade stealthily into the surf, trying to avoid detection by the Japanese, waves break against the camera's lens.

Another sequence presents Mitchum making a midnight raid on a Japanese supply hut to steal food to keep himself and his newfound colleague alive. Mitchum has blackened his face to escape detection so that only the whites of his frightened and alert eyes are visible in the tight close-up of his face. In the middle of his robbery, a group of enemy soldiers arrives and he is forced to remain perfectly immobile as they chatter away jovially (the Japanese dialogue seems as loquacious as the English words are spare). In the darkness a rat crawls across Mitchum's paralysed form but the danger of being discovered is greater than that of a rat bite so he does not move. The suspense is reminiscent of the gripping robbery in *The Asphalt Jungle*, but it is achieved through more economical means. Not a single word is spoken and nothing is at stake but a few cans of beans, but the tension on the screen equals that of the most spectacular caper films.

The beauty of *Heaven Knows, Mr. Allison* is all in what it is not. Kerr and Mitchum do not exchange flirtatious banter when the situation seems to encourage it; they do not become romantically attached as their friendship deepens. Mitchum is not discovered and forced to fight it out with the Japanese when they enter the shed in which he is hiding. And when ferocious fighting explodes between rival battleships offshore, the screen is not filled with flames and destruction; there are only ominous flashes and rumblings in the distant sky. The emotional climax comes not in a burst of words and hysterical gestures, but with the muffled sobs of Kerr during a rainstorm and a drunken Mitchum muttering simply, "If ya had to be a nun, why couldn't ya be old and ugly?" From its very beginning, the film catches an energy vibrating between its two immensely gifted stars and never loses it. That energy is never cluttered by spurious effects, wasted words, or useless gestures. It is a tribute to Huston's sensitivity that he knew such energy could be best communicated with restraint and simplicity. He clearly understood the wisdom of the advice offered by Mitchum in the film's first spoken words: "Let's just keep it quiet."

8

Bad Luck

IN 1957, JOHN HUSTON hit a run of bad luck. For most people accustomed to the ups and downs of the movie industry, there would have been nothing exceptional in that. But luck for Huston had begun to seem a natural right; for the better part of two decades, he had never been without it. From the beginning when he was teamed up with Bogart and assigned to a Dashiell Hammett story that virtually turned itself into a first-rate screenplay, his good fortune seemed inexhaustible. Ever since then if his material was good, as it was most notably with *Sierra Madre, The Asphalt Jungle, The Red Badge of Courage,* and *Moby Dick,* he triumphed. If it was a bit shaky, as it was with *Across the Pacific, We Were Strangers,* and *Heaven Knows, Mr. Allison,* he brought it to life anyway. And then there was the case of *Beat the Devil,* in which there was really no material at all and yet still the happy-go-lucky moviemaker landed deftly on his feet.

In the case of other directors' careers, survival and success may have come at the cost of methodical, tenacious struggle; for Huston, it seemed to have come almost by accident, as if to prove, as his father had said in *Sierra Madre,* that life itself was but "a great joke." Huston had always been able to laugh and to, in Melville's words, "take this whole universe for a vast practical joke." Somehow things had a way of turning out in his favor. Until 1957, that is. There were no dark portents, no evil signs, or evidence of some mysterious divine displeasure. Huston had not changed any of his working methods or, at least at first, in any way lessened the energy or relish he brought to his work. He simply ran out of his heretofore ever-present luck.

Upon completion of *Heaven Knows, Mr. Allison* (released to a well-deserved chorus of critical praise), Huston was offered an adaptation of the Hemingway novel *A Farewell to Arms* by producer David Selznick. Though they had never formally worked together, director and producer knew each other well and the former was wary of the latter's propensity for meddling in areas outside the producer's traditional do-

John Wayne as an early American emissary to Japan in The Barbarian and the Geisha. *Courtesy of the Museum of Modern Art, Film Stills Archive.*

89

main. Huston, nevertheless, accepted and made extensive preparations to begin shooting in the Italian Alps; but Selznick's interference
became insufferable, and Huston withdrew, leaving it to the compliant
Charles Vidor to finish the film that Huston wanted no part of. Perhaps
he was thankful for having escaped certain disaster by taking orders
from Selznick, but it was to prove small satisfaction compared to the
enormous frustrations that awaited him.

The Barbarian and the Geisha (1958)

As the second step in the fulfillment of his three-film contract with
20th Century-Fox, Huston took on a project that bore some of the
characteristics of his first. Like *Heaven Knows, Mr. Allison*, *The Townsend Harris Story* left plenty to be desired as a drama but was appealing in its locale. It purported to be an account of the first American
ambassador to Japan, one of the first Westerners to penetrate its
closed, tradition-bound society. In fact, the script as written by Fox
scenarist Charles Grayson had completely ignored historical fact and
dwelled on a romantic fiction—that the ambassador had had a passionate affair with a beautiful geisha girl. Again Huston overhauled the
script given him in collaboration with the author of the first draft, but
this time his efforts did not seem to improve things much. Nor could
the cast be looked to with much optimism; the principal performers
were unlikely to create the magic of the Mitchum-Kerr combination.
They were a grievously miscast John Wayne, supposed to be a wily
negotiator of international affairs, and a Japanese entertainer named
Eiko Ando, whose command of English was even weaker than the lum-
bering Wayne's credibility as a polished diplomat.

Huston appears to have approached the production with something
of the same mentality with which he had made *Moulin Rouge*, resigned
to the banality of the narrative and thereby free to concentrate solely
on the visual style. "I was always interested in Japanese art," he later
recalled, "and while I was shooting I was collecting. It was fascinating.
Making a picture in Japan is a very good way of going into the character
of the people. . . . I loved the period, and the settings, and imagining
what life in Japan was really like at that time."[1] Huston, at enormous
expense, busied himself with the details of art direction, ordering
thousands of artificial cherry blossoms hung on trees, turning a giant
convention hall into a facsimile of a shogun ruler's palace, staging long
ceremonial processions. Perhaps in the film's wandering, contempla-
tive pace, Huston imagined that he was respecting the rhythm and
structure of Japanese film, but for the occidental viewer, the result is
tedium, which arises because, to a greater degree even than in *Moulin
Rouge*, the story is without life.

The Roots of Heaven (1958)

It would be pleasing to report that, in keeping with *The Red Badge of Courage* parallel, Huston's escape to Africa was to result in a triumphant vindication of his talent when it was not interfered with. But *The Roots of Heaven* is only a marginally better film than its predecessor, and this time the director could not blame John Wayne.

The material came from a novel by French writer Romain Gary, published in 1956, about one man's widely publicized and politically disruptive crusade to protect African elephants in French colonial Chad. The novel is long and didactic, making its points about the endangered condition of African wildlife, the hypocrisy and pomposity of colonial administration, and the exploitative nature of the media with a heavy hand. Its author, however, was the French consul in Los Angeles and active on the Hollywood social circuit, so his book, with its timely theme, was well-promoted in the movie community. When Huston expressed an interest in it as the possible basis of the third film on his contract with Fox, the studio promptly bought it for him. Also interested in the property was Darryl Zanuck, who had left the top position at Fox on friendly terms to become an independent producer. Zanuck promised to be less meddlesome than the last strong-willed producer Huston had worked for, David O. Selznick. Other than asking that French actress Juliette Greco be employed, Zanuck imposed no constraints upon Huston and did all in his power to see that the director's will was done. Huston thus had enviable freedom (which he used at once to commission another version of the script from a writer named Patrick Leigh-Fermor, despite the fact that Zanuck had promised Gary that his version would not be tampered with). True to Huston form, the project was international in both its cast and shooting locations—the Cameroons, in what was then French Equatorial Africa, for exteriors and Paris for studio work. And still more promising, its story was equally in the Huston mold, dealing with the adventures of a group of eccentrics engaged in a seemingly hopeless quest.

The cast as well was a strong one. There was Trevor Howard as the man crazed with a missionary fervor about saving elephants, Juliette Greco looking sultry and erotic, if a bit out of place in the African wilds, Errol Flynn who, though in the final stages of fatal alcoholism, handled his role easily—thanks no doubt to the fact that it called for him to pretend to be in the final stages of fatal alcoholism. Orson Welles was again given a flamboyant cameo role that, like that in *Moby Dick*, did not require him to endure the rigors of location shooting but that, unlike it, seems not to have been undertaken with much ardor. The crew, including Oswald Morris as cinematographer and Stephen Grimes as art director, also met Huston's specifications. There is much in the film that is engaging to look at: the stampede of elephant herds, flocks of flamingos gathered under a multicolored sky, a raging sand-storm. The problem is that the story does not stir. The film has the same leaden pedantry as its source and the viewer wearies of its arguments long before it stops reiterating them.

If Huston had gone into retirement after *Heaven Knows, Mr. Allison*, there would have been an impeccable unity to his work, not just in themes—failed quests, laughing in the face of cruel fate—but in a passion, an energy brought to every project. He may have needed to keep directing for financial reasons, but the results had never seemed the work of someone on a routine assignment, bored with his job. Beginning with *The Barbarian and the Geisha*, however, the pattern changed. There were perhaps larger reasons, a general lack of verve in the weakened motion picture industry as a whole, that could explain why Huston began making, with disturbing frequency, mediocre films. The late fifties and early sixties can certainly be regarded as a dreary time for American cinema.

But the decline of John Huston cannot be explained solely by that of the industry in general. Nor does the evidence support any Ahab-like image of a too-proud artist who, having aimed too high, was brought down by an angry God. Huston in fact seemed to have lost none of his passion and talent; in the decades to come he was to make films (albeit only a few) that were every bit the equal of his best earlier work. What he lost was the ability or the willingness to apply those qualities every time he went to work. Whether for financial reasons or out of sheer inertia, Huston kept working even when his heart was not in it. Over the next twenty years he would find material that impassioned him and thrive on it, but more often he would simply go through the motions on whatever production had a high enough budget to pay his salary. For conservative producers wanting to avoid all risks, Huston's name was a safe one, so he never lacked for work.

The Unforgiven (1960)

That attitude surfaces frankly for the first time on the film that followed *The Roots of Heaven*, a Western called *The Unforgiven*. His contract with Fox terminated, Huston signed on to a project for the independent production firm that Burt Lancaster had formed with two partners, Harold Hecht and James Hill. Although the group thought of themselves as defiers of convention and achieved some prestige with *Marty* (1955), from a Paddy Chayevsky script and with an Oscar-winning performance by Ernest Borgnine in the title role, their stock-in-trade was the Western and their most exploited asset the brawling heroics of the actor-partner, Lancaster. Robert Aldrich had established

himself as a first-rate handler of big-screen action in two such adventures starring Lancaster, both released in 1954. In *Apache,* the star
played an Indian who learned the hard way that white men could not
be trusted; in the sprawling epic *Vera Cruz* he was a treacherous mer-
cenary for the Mexican emperor Maximilian. And Lancaster had directed himself as an intrepid Texas-bound pioneer in *The Kentuckian*
(1955). The emphasis in Hecht-Hill-Lancaster productions was on
Western action and, whatever nods were made to the world of ideas,
they surely had not given Huston much reason to believe otherwise.

What little hope he might have had that *The Unforgiven* held some
promise lay in his previous contact with the author of its script, Ben
Maddow, and its already hired cast. Huston had helped Maddow turn
W. R. Burnett's crime story into *The Asphalt Jungle.* But this time
Maddow was adapting far inferior material, a novel by Alan LeMay,
and Huston did not work with him: his contract with Hecht-Hill-Lancaster precluded changes in the script. Still the cast members, though
they, too, were already assembled when Huston was engaged, held
promise. There was Lancaster himself (who, as one of Huston's employers, was in the ironic position of preventing him from working on
the script when it had been Huston's talent as a writer on *The Killers*
that had helped launch Lancaster's career). He was joined by Audrey
Hepburn, fresh from winning performances in Billy Wilder's *Love in
the Afternoon* (1957) and Fred Zinneman's *The Nun's Story* (1959); Audie Murphy, veteran of wars both real and Huston-created; and the
agelessly beautiful star of D. W. Griffith's inaugural epic of the screen,
Lillian Gish. The location, too, should have helped inspire Huston:
the foothills of the Sierra Madre not far from the scene of his great
work with his father. But neither Maddow, the gifted cast, or the appealing location seemed to make much difference.

From the beginning of the shooting, Huston appears to have been
uncharacteristically apathetic. A journalist visiting the set reported
with admiration that he was "certainly one of the most relaxed directors in the business. Even during tense moments he is likely to be
sauntering among the spectators or gossiping with the crew. The director's chair, when he uses it, is a self-effacing distance from the action, usually at the edge of the circle of spectators."[2] The description
of Huston's behavior, as innocent as it seems, contrasts suspiciously
with accounts of his near-obsessional attention to detail on productions
he was enthusiastic about, and it directly contradicts John Wayne's
complaints about Huston's attitude during the shooting of *The Barbarian and the Geisha.* Clearly, this time it was the director who wished
he were somewhere else.

The story moves with annoying slowness at first, but its sluggishness
seems in retrospect preferable to the distasteful action that follows: a

The agelessly beautiful Lillian Gish returns to the Western in a determined pose in
The Unforgiven. *Courtesy of the Museum of Modern Art, Film Stills Archive.*

climactic gun battle against attacking Indians, as if genocide was a heroic goal and Audrey Hepburn and Lillian Gish were born killers. Not
only is the carnage grotesque; it seems indulged in meaninglessly as a
deliberate sacrilege against the gentle and intelligent screen images of
Hepburn and Gish. For once Huston is the best guide to his own work
when he says in his autobiography: "Some of my pictures I don't care
for, but *The Unforgiven* is the only one I actually dislike. . . . I
watched it on television one night recently, and after about half a reel
I had to turn the damn thing off. I couldn't bear it" (*OB*, 284).

9

Misfits

AFTER THREE UNINTERESTING failures, Huston's career may be said to have taken a turn for the better when, in 1960, he made an interesting failure. *The Misfits* is often clumsy in its staging, frequently pretentious in its dialogue, and has an unsatisfying dramatic structure. Yet in comparison to the tedium of *The Barbarian and the Geisha* and *The Roots of Heaven*, and the ugliness of *The Unforgiven*, its virtues stand out: it was obviously undertaken with sincerely high aspirations and strove toward admirable goals. Its failure was a far nobler one on Huston's part.

The idea grew out of a short story by playwright Arthur Miller. To obtain a divorce, he had established Nevada residency in a little town north of Reno and there met a group of cowboys who eked out a marginal living by flushing wild horses out of the mountains with a small plane, running them down in a truck, capturing them with lassos, and then selling them by the pound to be turned into dog food. The subject's appeal to the playwright who had always been fascinated with the ways men could devise to earn a living was strong: both the cowboys and their prey were endangered species, anachronistic vestiges of an extinct American frontier. Both, in relation to the modern world, were "misfits." Appearing under that title in *Esquire* magazine, Miller's story succeeded beautifully in evoking a sense of the Nevada landscape and the lives of three lonely drifters who had found in it a temporary peace. The material was to go through several incarnations, but none was as successful on its own terms as the first.

Not long after the story's publication, Arthur Miller married the actress who, since her small but provocative role in *The Asphalt Jungle*, had become one of the screen's supreme embodiments of female sexuality. For his wife, Marilyn Monroe, Miller expanded *The Misfits* into what he called a "cinema novel," a preliminary step to turning it into a screenplay. The new version took a female character who had figured only marginally in the original story and made her the centerpiece in the lives of the three men. It was, of course, Miller's intention that his wife play the role in the film. He sent the new "cinema novel" to John Huston, then finishing *The Roots of Heaven* in Paris, who pronounced it "magnificent" and expressed his desire to bring it to the screen. A few months later Miller was at Huston's Irish estate working with him on a screenplay.

The combination of great playwright, celebrated director, and ravishing star seemed to inspire confidence in everyone. The "king" of Hollywood, Clark Gable, expressed enthusiasm for the role of the eldest of the cowboy trio, which was then completed by Montgomery Clift and Eli Wallach. The salaries of the actors alone guaranteed that the production would be an expensive one, but the stellar names attracted backing with no difficulty. The aura surrounding *The Misfits* began when it was still on paper, then flourished while it was in production fanned by rumors suggesting that the Miller-Monroe marriage was on the rocks, that the star herself was falling apart, that Clift had been physically but not emotionally repaired after a terrible car accident and that yet, despite all this, Clark Gable considered the film the best thing he had ever been involved with. The aura was to reach its zenith several years later when it became clear that death had been lying in wait for three of the film's four main performers. Gable died before the film was released, Monroe a year and a half after it, and Clift just a few years later. The myth of *The Misfits* transcended the work of Miller and Huston.

Despite its flourishing myth, there is an emptiness about the actual film. The actors' charisma so towers over the story they are supposed to enact that the viewer is kept waiting for extraordinary moments that never come. What is heard instead are lines that strain too hard for profundity, that overplay a sense of futility and despair. Among them are such pronouncements as: "The trouble is I always end up back where I started." "Everything just happened wrong." "We're all dying, aren't we? And we aren't teaching each other what we really know, are we?" "What's eating you?—Just my life." "We're all blind bombardiers, killing people we never saw." "Nothing can live unless something dies." The lines are not expressive of the personalities of individual characters; the spokesmen for Miller's platitudes seem interchangeable. Nor are they of much help in advancing the story; on the contrary, action always seems to defer to message, allowing it center stage. There is a morbid fascination to watching the legendary Gable, the intense, emotionally disturbed Clift, and the doomed love goddess Monroe, all drawing near the end of their lives, but they are not gainfully employed. As in the last film Huston had drawn from the work of a famous playwright, Maxwell Anderson's *Key Largo*, the drama is laden with talent but overwritten.

But even if it is incapable of fulfilling the expectations it stirs, *The*

Misfits still has its moments. Shooting on American soil for the first time since *The Red Badge of Courage*, and with a cinematographer, Russell Metty, veteran of *We Were Strangers*, who in his work for directors as disparate as Orson Welles and Douglas Sirk, had proved superbly adaptable to directors' individual visions, Huston captured images that live in a way the drama does not. In Monroe's strange drunken dance in the desert moonlight, the ambience of rowdy barrooms at rodeo time, aerial views of a wild desert landscape, galloping horses shot from a low-flying plane, and most memorable of all, the final chasing down of mustangs in a flatbed truck, there is a poetry without words. Metty's camera seems to move across the endless salt flats with the abandon of the wild stallion it is focused on. The precarious high-speed attempt to lasso the horses, their furious but futile attempts to keep on while dragging the old tires to which the end of the lasso has been secured, and the final subjugation of the entangled beasts, are as stirring an example of action filmmaking as Huston had done since the rousing maritime battles of *Moby Dick*. The spare but powerful impact of such scenes recalls those same qualities in Miller's original story and encourages wistful speculation about what *The Misfits* might have been if it had not been weighted down by its celebrity cast and Miller's compulsion to embalm it in pseudoprofundity.

The repeated frustrations of working with mediocre or ill-conceived scripts might well have made Huston cynical or apathetic about his work. He had reason to conclude that in the movie business artistic scruples were a handicap and that the path of least resistance was to take on whatever assignment offered high pay and agreeable working conditions and to leave questions of art to the critics. That in effect was what he seemed to have done with *The Unforgiven*, and the trying experience of working with a deteriorating Monroe, while her husband overwrote his script, could scarcely have made further risk-taking attractive. But of all the faults of which Huston could be accused, predictability was never among them. His next project was one of the bravest and least conventional of his career. *Freud* is the first of a number of altogether unexpected testaments to the fact that, however many undistinguished films intervened, Huston was always capable of suddenly returning to his finest form.

Freud (1962)

Huston had been tossing about the idea of a biographical treatment of Sigmund Freud for a long time. During the thirties, Warner Brothers, where he was working, had developed something of a specialized genre: fictionalized biographies of famous men. Huston had had a hand in the script of several of them, *Juarez* (1938), *Dr. Ehrlich's Magic*

Clark Gable and Montgomery Clift in the memorable final chase scene of the mustangs in The Misfits. *Courtesy of the Museum of Modern Art, Film Stills Archive.*

Bullet (1940), and *Sergeant York* (1941). At the time, Huston had discussed with a fellow Warners scenarist, Wolfgang Reinhardt (brother of Gottfried, the hero-producer of *The Red Badge of Courage*), the possibility of a film about the father of psychoanalysis. Huston's career at Warners had been disrupted by the war but he emerged from it with an even deeper interest in the subject. During the making of the climactic chapter of his war trilogy, *Let There Be Light,* Huston's interest in the treatment of psychiatric disorders became more than that of just a screenwriter in search of a popular subject. In the wards of Mason General Hospital his education really began. "I got a short course in psychiatry there, the best advice instantly available," he recalled. "I read, crammed as it were, all the time I was there making the film. I knew nothing about the subject, I'd read a little Freud like everyone else but only superficially, and I had a vague idea of what he was about, but working there his figure loomed large at every turn. His presence was always felt and it was the name uttered oftener than anyone else's."[1] When, in the interval between *The Roots of Heaven* and *The Unforgiven,* Reinhardt again raised the idea of a film on

Freud, Huston resolved to do it. And he knew just who should prepare the script: Jean-Paul Sartre.

The flamboyant movie director and the erudite philosopher and writer were strange bedfellows, but their rapport was genuine. Just after finishing *Let There Be Light* and before returning to commercial moviemaking, Huston had directed the American premiere of Sartre's play, *Huis Clos.* Six years later, in 1952, during the production of *Moulin Rouge* in Paris, the two had met and exchanged professions of mutual respect. Sartre, in Huston's view, combined the ability to dramatize abstract ideas with a deep understanding of Freud's theories. As soon as Huston was able to shake himself free from his unhappy work on *The Unforgiven*, he retreated to his Irish manor and he and Sartre began lengthy discussions on the nature of the Freud project. By the time Huston departed for Nevada and *The Misfits*, Sartre had finished a voluminous script that if filmed would have been eight hours long. When *The Misfits* was finished, Huston was able to line up backing for the production of *Freud* from Universal Pictures, but only on the condition that it have a conventional running time. At least two more versions of the script then followed. Huston first tried working with Charles Kaufman, who had worked with him on *Let There Be Light*, and then with the man with whom he had first conceived the idea, Wolfgang Reinhardt. The result was a hybrid—work done by Sartre, who took no official credit, combined with that by Kaufman and Reinhardt, who did. Together their efforts somehow accomplished Huston's seemingly contradictory goal: *Freud* was to become an intellectual thriller.

The film begins with Huston's own magisterial voice asserting that "since ancient times, there have been three great changes in man's conception of himself." Copernicus, he explains, informed men that their world was not flat, Darwin that they were descended from beasts, and Freud that they led an unconscious life over which their rational self was powerless. One may balk at such a sweeping summation of human history, but the momentous tone of Huston's words succeeds in arousing the viewer's interest. Then he announces his intention to embark on "a descent into a region almost as dark as hell itself—man's unconscious." The ponderous nature of such a subject could, with very little mishandling, veer into the ridiculous, but it does not.

The scene is Vienna in 1885 but it is strikingly similar to Mason General Hospital in 1945. It is the story of how Freud "let in the light" that was passed on to the doctors of *Let There Be Light*. The patients in the fictional Austrian hospital are, like the real traumatized soldiers back from the war, suffering from problems that have no obvious medical cause. Again, hypnosis proves useful in delving into the patients' pasts for answers. But, unlike the documentary that helped inspire it,

this Huston essay on the troubles of the mind implies that those answers can be infernally hard to ferret out and, for those tortured by
their own minds, happy rehabilitation after a couple of months' treatment is not, as the film for the army seemed to imply, the inevitable
result of psychoanalysis. And consistent with that difference in message is the contrast between the benignly competent air of the doctors
at Mason General and the intense, uncertain air of the man portraying
Sigmund Freud, Montgomery Clift.

The casting of Clift was an act Huston regretted soon after shooting
started; the actor's mental health had been precarious during the making of *The Misfits,* but stable enough to encourage Huston to gamble
on his being able to make another film. But it soon appeared that he
was wrong; Clift's behavior worsened. In addition to alcohol and drug
problems, he was going blind. He could neither do very well at mem-
orizing his lines nor at reading them if they were put in front of him
on the set. He was, said Huston, "very, very hard to work with." With
what could be considered an impossibly complicated and ambitious
subject and the film's single most important actor often incapacitated,
disaster should have ensued. Instead, Huston was reunited with an old
friend: luck.

Clift's condition may have made him a nightmare to work with, but
his haunted, troubled appearance, which had seemed just another
anomaly in *The Misfits,* now seemed absolutely appropriate to the portrayal of Freud. The interior tension, the unmistakable signs of deep
psychic pain, had less to do with acting technique than with Clift's real
problems, giving him unintentionally much in common with the patients interviewed in *Let There Be Light.* His intensity is not only credible, but frightening for it seems inconceivable that he will be able to
shed it when the cameras stop turning and he walks off the set. And it
gives his reflections a sincerity and power an actor more in control of
himself would not likely have had. He seems really to mean it, for
example, when as Freud, just after a vivid nightmare, he asks himself
"Could it be that dreams are ideas escaping from repression in
disguise?"

The film's structure is that of a suspenseful detective tale in which
Freud, in spite of the skepticism of his medical colleagues, attempts
to discover the source of torments buried in the unconscious both of
his patients and of himself. Effectively staged dream sequences take
the viewer into the minds of a neurotic young man (played by David
McCallum) obsessed with his mother, and an equally disturbed woman
(Susannah York), whose troubles are with her father. In the classic
manner of detective fiction, the pursuit of the truth is impeded by
misleading clues and leads that become dead ends, but Freud remains
intrepid and persistent. The stakes are more than high enough to sus-

tain suspense: if Freud does not solve his mysteries quickly enough, madness and suicide will prevail. No two-hour movie whose primary duty was to capture the interest of a general audience could ever, of course, function as a definitive account of Freud's theories on psychoanalysis. Huston's film inevitably took liberties with the biographical facts and simplified Freud's ideas. But those liberties were not undertaken with fraudulent intent nor did the simplification mean trivialization. That Clift's problems worked to the film's benefit may have been lucky, but combining respect for the intellectual achievements of a complicated genius with lively suspenseful moviemaking was a matter of talent. After a string of disappointments, Huston proved he still had it.

10

Menagerie

FOUR FILMS AND five years had intervened between *Heaven Knows, Mr. Allison* and *Freud*. Curiously, exactly the same interval was then to elapse between the latter and Huston's next fully satisfying film, *Reflections in a Golden Eye* (1967). None of his works of the middle sixties was as boring as *The Barbarian and the Geisha* or as offensive as *The Unforgiven*, but neither does any of them reward very close scrutiny. The first was *The List of Adrian Messenger*, a murder mystery that, uncharacteristically for Huston, managed to be far less involving than its literary source.

The List of Adrian Messenger (1963)

Philip MacDonald's 1959 novel of the same title is no literary landmark, but it unrolls wittily and suspensefully within the traditional boundaries of mystery fiction. Its characters are appealing and well delineated, the rhythm of its telling nicely modulated, and its denouement suitably dramatic. Generally, given such qualities in his literary source, Huston could be expected to translate them to the screen. But perhaps disinclined to exert himself fully after the tribulations of *Freud*, he gives the material a frivolous treatment, changing it in ways that appeared to have more to do with his life as an Irish country squire than a desire to bring life to his story.

The fact that MacDonald's book had not been set in Ireland and had had nothing to do with fox hunting was no impediment to Huston and his veteran script collaborator, Anthony Veiller. They steered the script straight into the milieu where the director himself preferred to live (and where he could afford to live only because of his willingness to keep working without regard for his enthusiasm for his material). Within minutes, *The List of Adrian Messenger* escapes the glum buildings of London where most of the book had transpired and is sweeping across the Irish countryside. There is talk of the film's ostensible subject, "a mass murder plot so preposterous as to deny belief," but it

ohn Huston directs himself as Noah in The Bible . . . In he Beginning. *Courtesy of the Museum of Modern Art, ilm Stills Archive.*

105

somehow pales before the spectacle of beautiful thoroughbreds leaping rock walls, racing across open meadows and through forest glens. The conservationist militancy of *The Roots of Heaven* has long been forgotten; the message here is "it is man's nature to hunt, it is the fox's to be hunted." The film's villain is guilty not only of ruthless mass murder, but, even worse, of taking part in a demonstration against fox hunting. How, the viewer is encouraged to wonder, during the exciting ground-level tracking shots of hounds running and horses jumping, could even a murderer sink so low?

The film's other source of amusement lies in a continuous game of masquerade, which has a vague connection to the book, whose villain assumed several disguises. But Huston takes the game much further. Not only is its villain, Kirk Douglas, made to assume a variety of outlandish identities, but somehow Robert Mitchum, Burt Lancaster, Frank Sinatra, and Tony Curtis, are all snuck before the cameras so thoroughly camouflaged by the make-up artist that only at the film's end is the viewer coyly let in on the joke. It is a joke with no relevance to the story, which, quite independently, reached its conclusion a few minutes earlier with, not surprisingly, a fox hunt and a hound as the ultimate detective hero.

Huston's flippant self-indulgence did not bother anyone at the studio that was paying for it, Universal. "I didn't have any difficulty with the studio over it," he recalled. "That's the sort of picture they leave alone. . . . It's usually different if you want to do something a little out-of-the-ordinary."[1] For the moment, the director was content to plod on without ruffling any feathers and there was nothing "out-of-the-ordinary" about his next project either. *The Night of the Iguana* was a film version of an already tested play by an established playwright, Tennessee Williams, staffed by celebrities whose names insured press attention and box office success: Ava Gardner, Richard Burton, Deborah Kerr, and the nymphette star of Stanley Kubrick's *Lolita* (1962), Sue Lyon. The Mexican location was so much to the director's taste that he was later to make his home there. Perhaps this was his strongest incentive for his accepting the assignment.

The Night of the Iguana (1964)

Williams had set his play "in a rather rustic and very Bohemian hotel, the Costa Verde, which as its name implies, sits on a jungle-covered hilltop overlooking the 'caleta' or 'morning beach' of Puerto Barrio." His introduction to the play goes on to describe the setting as "on the west coast of Mexico" and "among the world's wildest and loveliest populated places." Huston's love of Mexico was long-standing; besides being the scene of his postwar triumph, *The Treasure of the Sierra Madre*, he had arranged to shoot *The Unforgiven* there and planned, until overruled by Arthur Miller, to stay there to make *The Misfits*. An architect friend had helped him find a remote locale as wild and lovely as Williams's play called for, a place where, as the director described it, there was "a long, wide, sandy beach, and a jungly-overgrown tongue of land jutted out into the sea. The view from the top of this point—clear on three sides—was spectacular." Huston arranged for his art director Stephen Grimes to construct a "rather rustic and very Bohemian hotel" as well as accommodations for his cast and crew (*OB*, 308).

With colorful celebrities stirring up free publicity ("We've got more reporters here than iguanas," reportedly gloated producer Ray Stark),[2] a script that for the most part simply followed the play, and a lovely setting, Huston's job was far from demanding. "Offhand I would say it is the easiest picture I have done in years, maybe in all the years. It is almost too easy,"[3] he told one of the swarming reporters. What exactly he meant by "too easy" is not clear, but he could well have been referring to the near-anonymity of his position. *The Night of the Iguana* is little more than a Tennessee Williams play photographically record-ed. The modifications Huston and Veiller made in the script are, ex-cept for a comic opening sequence that is the liveliest part of the film, inconsequential and very little effort is made to exploit the fact that the action was not restricted to a stage. The actors speak their lines; the camera and microphone record them. A lesser director might have worked a little slower or missed a few small touches, but the result would not have been much different. Huston's presence is largely invisible.

The problem with recording a stage play on film with little alteration is that the stylization that can be accepted on the stage as dramatic license seems self-conscious and fake on the screen. Williams's char-acters are long on eccentric posturing and short on flesh and blood. Although their language is more colloquial than that of the characters in Maxwell Anderson's *Key Largo*, Huston's previous adaptation from the stage, he and Richard Brooks went much farther in the previous film in bringing the characters to life. Perhaps precisely because Wil-liams's play was a bigger success to begin with, Huston, again working with Anthony Veiller, felt less compelled to change it. In any case, Burton's tortured, alcoholic ex-priest, Gardner's bitchy, carnal hotel proprietor, and Kerr's chaste and poetic artist, seem to be playing to the farthest back rows on Broadway instead of to a camera right in front of their noses in remotest Mexico. The result is disagreeable.

After *The Night of the Iguana*, which suffered from claustrophobia and too much talk, Huston bolted wildly to the other extreme as if in compensation. From the enclosed theatrical world of Tennessee Williams, he moved to a gargantuan spectacle that had cameras turning all over the globe. At the request of Italian producer Dino De Laurentiis, who thrived on announcing outlandishly ambitious projects, raising millions of dollars for their production, and then hoping that the snowballing publicity would attract enough moviegoers to pay for whatever resulted, Huston agreed to direct *The Bible*.

The Bible . . . In the Beginning (1966)

De Laurentiis's first announced idea about bringing Christianity's fundamental document to the screen had such a lunatic grandeur to it that it is impossible not to fantasize about what it would have been like. In 1961, the producer modestly informed the press of his intention to begin "the greatest project ever attempted in motion picture history," a movie that would "cancel out all other films on the Bible." Estimates on the budget varied, depending on when he was asked, from forty to ninety million dollars and the running time would be about twelve hours. No single director, De Laurentiis admitted, could handle such a responsibility on his own, so the work was to be parceled out to five of the world's greatest directors, Orson Welles, Robert Bresson, Federico Fellini, Luchino Visconti, and John Huston. Igor Stravinsky was to compose an original score and Laurence Olivier was to prepare himself for the role of God. A gigantic block-long billboard in Times Square kept the public aware of De Laurentiis's plans.

But as first months and then years went by with only a billboard as testament to his vision, the producer grudgingly admitted that "there's been a little trouble." The trouble was that, with the exception of Huston, none of the above-named eminences wanted anything to do with the project. Nor, it seemed, did anyone want to put up the money to pay for it. Only Huston seemed to respond positively to De Laurentiis's bravado, so, three years after its publicity campaign had begun, *The Bible* actually began production with Huston alone at the helm. Undaunted by the scaling down of his plans, De Laurentiis kept the impressive statistics flowing.

Thousands of young ladies around the world were considered for the role of Eve, ten thousand costumes were designed for as many cast members. One set alone occupied twenty-five acres; Noah's ark was, of course, built to scale, 200 feet long by 60 feet high. Its contents occasioned another deluge of numbers: no less than 200 species assembled in pairs whose daily diet was proudly reported to consist of 1,320 pounds of hay, 638 pounds of fresh meat and poultry, 330 pounds of oats, 878 pounds of vegetables, and 357 pounds of fruit. Somewhere between the 10,000 costumes and 1,320 pounds of hay, while the budget mounted to 18 million dollars and crews shuttled between Mount Vesuvius and the Sahara Desert, was the director who had once made an involving, fully realized motion picture drama with one actor, Robert Mitchum, one actress, Deborah Kerr, and a short stretch of beach.

The Bible promised to be a plodding succession of lavish tableaux, strong on production values, but too pious and highly financed to be able to afford any spontaneous feeling. It fulfilled its every promise. So dwarfed by the scale of the thing, Huston's talents are in general even less discernible than in the filmed record of Williams's play; but two sections of the spectacle deserve at least a passing mention: its opening sequence depicting the creation of the universe, and the story of Noah's ark. To the former Huston contributed only his voice and his financial support; the latter is an appealing combination of mammoth spectacle and ingenuous home movie.

The creation sequence was the work of still photographer Ernst Haas, whose studies of the natural world had caught Huston's eye. Haas was commissioned to set out for the wildest corners of the globe and capture with a movie camera scenes of primordial beauty. His travels covered several continents touching down in such spots as Iceland and the Galapagos Islands in search of the primeval. In keeping with the spirit of munificence that was the production's hallmark, Haas's work, though it was to be on the screen for just a minute or two, reportedly cost a quarter of a million dollars. The issue of cost-efficiency aside however, *The Bible*'s first few minutes are genuinely striking. As Huston's grave voice begins to read from the opening verses of Genesis, the screen is black. But as he reaches the point where "God said 'let there be light' and there was light," the 70 millimeter frame explodes into pure white light. Then follow Haas's brooding images of roaring waters, volcanic upheaval, and turbulent skies. For a precious few minutes, until a blond Aryan type (actor Michael Parks) is introduced as Adam, his nudity coyly masked, there is the excitement of seeing the largest of film formats consecrated to pure color and rhythm, a brief glimpse of what might happen if the medium's most overwhelming format was freed of its obligations to narrative and became the plaything of a visual artist.

The sequence is, by necessity, frustratingly brief, however, for, even limiting itself to just the book of Genesis, *The Bible* had a lot of ground to cover. Adam and Eve must leave Eden, Cain must kill Abel, the world must be destroyed in a flood, the Tower of Babel must be constructed, Abraham and Sarah must bear a child, and Sodom must be destroyed. All of this is dutifully enacted by such stars as George C. Scott, Ava Gardner, and Peter O'Toole, but there is not much room for suspense or excitement. With the exception of Haas's prelude and the flood story, only the scale, and at times some impressive art direction, catch the eye.

After failing to obtain the services of either his first choice, Charlie Chaplin, or his second, Alec Guiness, the director decided to cast himself in the role of Noah. It was not his debut as an actor; he had had a few bit roles in his predirectorial days, a cameo in *Sierra Madre* and then, in the interval between *The List of Adrian Messenger* and *The Night of the Iguana*, he had taken a part in Otto Preminger's *The Cardinal* (1963) where he had made such a distinctive impression as a curmudgeonly churchman that he had been nominated for a supporting actor Oscar. His effectiveness as a surly if not outrightly dastardly type on the screen was to win him increasingly frequent acting work during the next decade, which he readily accepted, always pleased at the prospect of collecting fees that often rivaled his director's pay for a lot less work. But there was nothing surly or dastardly about the self-imposed role of Noah. Looking uncannily like his father in *Sierra Madre* and behaving with something of the same combination of folksy humility and dogged determination, he sets about constructing his ark and assembling its living cargo.

What follows is interesting in two ways: on the surface it is a triumph of animal training—an extraordinary procession of zebras, elephants, giraffes, camels, ostriches, bears, llamas, rabbits, and goats, stretching to the horizon and marching placidly in line—that touchingly bears witness to Huston's genuine affinity for animals. As he gently shows his last passenger, a sublimely unhurried tortoise, on board, the effect is of a curiously personal glimpse of the man himself right in the midst of one of his most impersonal movies. The other intriguing aspect of the Huston/Noah story is the way it seems to mockingly echo the theme that critics have been most eager to define as the central one of his career: that of the eccentric engaged in an impossible quest. Besides the figure of his father as the jovially obsessed prospector seeking fabulous wealth, there is John Garfield seeking to overthrow a government, gangster Sterling Hayden seeking to acquire a horse farm, river rat Humphrey Bogart seeking to defeat the kaiser in Africa, and Gregory Peck seeking the death of a giant whale. Noah, with his harebrained scheme for saving every species on earth from extinction, is the ultimate Huston eccentric striving toward the most impossible goal. The premise is a bit silly, as is the happy ending in which the proud skipper bids his diverse cargo good-bye. But the story, after all, was not devised by Huston. The sequence is as close to self-expression as the huge anonymous pageant of *The Bible* ever comes.

Casino Royale (1967)

It is anonymity that prevails again, though in a far less dignified way, in the next film with which Huston was associated, *Casino Royale*. A satire on the James Bond series of adventure films that was garish, abrasive, and only occasionally funny (mostly when the camera was on Woody Allen playing "little Jimmy Bond"), the production was the work of a number of directors. Huston directed only the opening sequence and it bears his stamp in the same way that *The List of Adrian Messenger* did: it provided him with a pretext for celebrating the pleasures of the hunt and life on a country estate. It was not, any more than its immediate predecessors had been, a Huston film worthy of the name.

11

Fat City

Reflections in a Golden Eye (1967)

"THERE IS A FORT in the South where a few years ago a murder was committed," begins a short novel by Carson McCullers and a film by John Huston. The novel was first published in 1941, the year Huston directed his first film, a work whose success lay in its ability to translate the intensity of a book to the screen. Now, twenty-six years later, after considerable ups and downs, most recently downs, in the quality of his work, he brought all of the same virtues to *Reflections in a Golden Eye* that he had brought to *The Maltese Falcon*. Those virtues included an ability to present a very strange world in a very credible way, an adept handling of a perfectly chosen cast, and a control of pace and rhythm that fit the content flawlessly. Nearing the end of his third decade in the uncertain world of commercial moviemaking, Huston made his twenty-fifth film as compelling as his first.

To be sure, many things had changed between the early forties and the late sixties both in what went on the screen and how it got there. The reign of the Production Code was over; never, for example, would it have allowed a frank treatment of the homosexuality that Dashiell Hammett had implied in the characters played by Sydney Greenstreet, Peter Lorre, and Elisha Cook, Jr., in *The Maltese Falcon*. Without its demise, no treatment of McCullers's story, one of whose central concerns was that previously taboo subject, would have had any integrity. And gone the way of the Production Code was the huge factorylike studio system that had sponsored it. Huston was no longer a salaried employee of Warner Brothers but a free agent who signed on to one project at a time, negotiating with producers who were themselves often free agents who contracted with studios on a film-by-film basis, bargaining for financing in exchange for distribution rights.

The producer behind *Reflections in a Golden Eye* was Ray Stark, who had produced and hired Huston to direct *The Night of the Iguana*. If it was one of the director's less interesting works, that was probably

Tense moments: (top) Marlon Brando in Reflections in a Golden Eye; *(bottom) Stacy Keach and Jeff Bridges in* Fat City. *Courtesy of the Museum of Modern Art, Film Stills Archive.*

of little concern to Stark for it was also one of his more profitable. Though McCullers was not a celebrity on the scale of Tennessee Williams, there were still encouraging similarities: both were respected Southern writers whose work examined passion and repression. Stark purchased the rights to McCullers's second novel (her first, *The Heart Is a Lonely Hunter*, was not brought to the screen until a year later, in 1968, though her third, *The Member of the Wedding*, had enjoyed great success as both a Broadway play and then a film released in 1952) and gave the project to Huston, who had a great admiration for the author's work. Since the director had been dutiful and efficient in managing his last work with Stark, the producer once again granted him a large measure of control.

For the first draft of a screenplay Huston went to a Scottish novelist, Chapman Mortimer, who, like James Agee and Ray Bradbury before him, was not chosen because of any screenwriting experience but because of the director's fondness for his other work. When he read Mortimer's script, Huston was, he later said, "delighted with what he had written," and passed it on to McCullers herself for approval. That, after some discussion with Huston, was granted, and a final version taking into account the author's suggestions was then prepared by the director and his assistant Gladys Hill. Casting proved neither more troublesome nor less auspicious; Marlon Brando, Elizabeth Taylor, Julie Harris, and Brian Keith were signed to the principal roles. Ever loath to shoot on American soil, Huston arranged for McCullers's unnamed army base in the American South to be simulated under the guidance of Stephen Grimes within a studio in Rome. The Italian technicians who had been up to the demands of *The Bible* could hardly have been taxed by the simple requirements of Huston's far more modestly scaled project.

In dramatic contrast to the first Huston-Stark production, in which talk was florid but the action listless, *Reflections in a Golden Eye* is sparing in its dialogue, but advances in mysterious bursts of action that have the logic and inevitability of a dream. The dream is spun from the personalities of two intense and neurotic characters embodied by Marlon Brando and Julie Harris and their respective descents into their private worlds. Both performers bring to their parts echoes of previous roles that inform and enrich their embodiment of McCullers's world.

It was Elia Kazan's film version of Tennessee Williams's *A Streetcar Named Desire* (1952) that launched Brando. In that film and his other principal ones, such as *The Wild One* (1954) and *On the Waterfront* (1954), his volatility had found physical release in the course of the drama. But in McCullers's story, Huston reveals his volatile temperament in a context that allows it no cathartic release. Internalized, it becomes ever more dangerous and creates a nerve-wracking uncertainty as to where and when the inevitable breaking point will come. Then juxtaposed with Brando's repressed neuroses are those of Julie Harris, which are so close to the surface that they spill out in abundance at every opportunity. Her performance also gives a strange twist to the screen persona she had established as a sensitive introvert in the world of McCullers's *The Member of the Wedding* and then in Kazan's film of John Steinbeck's *East of Eden* (1955). This time her psychotic behavior is not at all veiled by a veneer of stability. By turning Brando's explosiveness in on itself and Harris's introversion outward, *Reflections in a Golden Eye* creates two contrasting forces, each so forceful it could have been the drama's center. Serving as a kind of buffer between the two and struggling to lend some credence to the ironic first line of McCullers's story, which asserts that "an Army post in peacetime is a dull place," are Elizabeth Taylor and Brian Keith as the spouses of Brando and Harris. Their adulterous liaison could likewise have served as the story's main subject, but it is a measure of the film's richness and of Huston's sense of balance that no single aspect of the story steals the show. Too many things of perverse fascination are going on at once.

Another source of satisfaction to a follower of Huston's career is the film's exciting and, finally, thoroughly appropriate use of the equestrian world. His personal fondness for horses had often been reflected in his films, but with an uneven degree of relevance to his larger purposes. Retiring to a horse farm had been the dream of the hero of *The Asphalt Jungle*. Right afterward cavalry warfare had played a part in *The Red Badge of Courage*, a film Huston had wanted to direct on horseback. Afternoons at the racetrack were presented as among the few happy times in the unhappy life of Toulouse-Lautrec in *Moulin Rouge* and the capture of wild horses had not only borne considerable metaphorical weight but had provided the liveliest action in *The Misfits*. More spurious were the celebrations of horsemanship and fox hunting in *The List of Adrian Messenger*.

But as Huston's camera tracks across meadows following the galloping mounts of Elizabeth Taylor and Brian Keith, he was not just indulging himself; riding horses was an integral part of McCullers's tale. With the exception of Harris, whose sanity is a lost cause from the start, the main characters' mental health is directly proportional to how well they ride. The only mildly troubled Keith is a good horseman, but Taylor, who alone is untouched by the neuroses around her, is even better. Brando's hold on himself is exactly as uncertain as his position in the saddle, and McCullers condensed his entire personality into a description of it: "He sat rigid as a ramrod in the exact position taught by the riding master. Perhaps he would not have ridden at all if he could have seen himself from the rear." It is no coincidence that it is in trying to ride his wife's stallion that Brando's character finally comes unglued, nor that his repressed passion is for the horse-loving stable-hand who finally takes the animal in hand. The sequence of Brando's fateful ride, a pivotal one in the film, directly follows Taylor's unhelpful advice to the bedridden Harris: "Whenever I get sick, I get on a horse and ride myself better." The line is not in the book but is absolutely true to it. As Brando saddles up the stallion, moves out of the corral, spurs the animal into a wild gallop, and then loses control of him, the camera follows him as fluidly as if it had an equally spirited mount of its own. The scenes evince the virtuosity of a director with not only a genuine passion for his subject but with an equally genuine artistic motive for its inclusion. Huston's love for the physical thrill of being on a horse, so long an important part of his play, now rendered a major service to his work.

The strengths of *Reflections in a Golden Eye* are those of all of Huston's best films. It captures the spirit of a good piece of literature through casting and performances so appropriate as to suggest the original author had written with just those actors in mind. When it departs from its source, it is never to betray it but to preserve a fidelity to it in another medium. There are no wasted words, gestures, or shots; the visual style is engrossing but not distracting. Huston was disappointed that most prints of the film did not have the golden tint he and Technicolor technicians in Italy had painstakingly perfected to match the work's mood. But even in its conventional color form, it fully merits his description of it as "one of my best pictures."

It is the critic's natural instinct to search for patterns in an artist's work and many of the greatest film directors have been very obliging in their consistency. In the case of John Ford, Alfred Hitchcock, or Howard Hawks, certain themes, ideas, even actors, seem to link each film solidly to another. But the movies of John Huston offer few opportunities for categorization. One can sometimes cite isolated connections—eccentrics on doomed quests, love of horses and Irish country life—or, more cynically, a breakdown might be made between pictures done for love and pictures done for money. But in general his films doggedly defy classification and have in common only their unfailing dissimilarity.

Sooner or later, even the most category-minded of critics must give up and consign Huston to the purgatory of unpredictability. *Reflections in a Golden Eye* was a serious film but it was not on a large scale; its successor was on a far grander scale but without a trace of seriousness. Nor happily were there the obligatory four failures before Huston's next major achievement, *Fat City* (1972). In fact, it was preceded by only three films and none of them is without interest. Neither *Sinful Davey* (1968), *A Walk with Love and Death* (1969), nor *The Kremlin*

Letter (1969) entirely deserved the critical and popular cold shoulder they all received.

Sinful Davey (1968)

Huston approached *Sinful Davey* in the same spirit he had brought to *The List of Adrian Messenger*: "I thought of it as just a lark and a romp, a sort of prank, which I could make entirely in Ireland," he later remarked.[1] But this time the lark did not conspire against the character of the story; the spirit of prankishness was inherent in the material to begin with. The source was a diary of a young Scotsman named David Haggart, which was worked into a script by James Webb and told a picaresque tale about an early-nineteenth-century rogue. The fanciful premise is that the young man has resolved to honor the memory of his father, who has been hanged as a thief, by surpassing his crimes. There follow ninety minutes of unrelenting activity that allow Huston to indulge in his taste for ribald humor, daring horsemanship, the Irish countryside, and the easygoing life of the landed gentry. Those elements had been part of *Adrian Messenger* and his section of *Casino Royale*, but they had been arbitrarily imposed. This time they were endemic.

Exuberantly played by John Hurt, the title character deserts from the king's army, robs from a pickpocket, is bombarded with potatoes by outraged townspeople, falls off a roof into a chicken coop, then into a pigsty, overturns a fish merchant's table, is covered in flour, liberates a herd of cattle from their pen, then dives through a window, all the while informing the viewer that "my mind was working like lightning; the mark of genius was to pluck profit from disaster." He falls into the hands of a doctor who is short on cadavers for his experiments and sees in him a promising specimen; his lightning-fast mind proposes robbing a grave instead, but before he can deliver the stolen corpse, he is arrested for body snatching and thrown in jail. But in *Sinful Davey's* world even a jail is a scene of merriment: Davey and his fellow inmates break through the floor separating them from their female counterparts, one of whom promptly suggests a party to "celebrate twenty years a whore." "The good book," points out one of the celebrants "was writ before sinners realized what real sinnin' could be."

In addition to the pleasure of watching Huston at play is the welcome reappearance in his world of the man seen too briefly in *The African Queen* and mercifully often in *Beat the Devil*, Robert Morley. In the fifteen years since the latter film, Morley has become still more grandly ridiculous. As the august Duke of Argyle, he is introduced as a referee of a horse race, promising a "keg of ale to every winner unless of course the judges have drunk it first." As the host of a grand ball,

he arranges for Davey to burglarize his guests after warning the local
constable to keep an eye on his wife's relatives. When Hurt is arrested
for the crime, Morley intercedes on his behalf explaining that "he re-
lieved my boredom, cost me nothing, and my wife hasn't thrown a ball
since."

Though Huston later complained bitterly about changes the producers made in the film, accusing them of ruining it just as *The Barbarian
and the Geisha* had been ruined, it remains an appealing film just as
the latter seemed destined not to be. Before being "ruined," *Sinful
Davey*, Huston claimed, was "easy and light, quick and refreshing and
delightful."[2] In all deference to his indignation, the same can be said
for the version that reached the screen.

A Walk with Love and Death (1969)

More debilitating problems plagued Huston's next project, problems he could not ascribe to others. *A Walk with Love and Death* is a
more ambitious production than its predecessor and one on which the
director encountered no interference; in many ways it is more impressive. Its premises are far more thought-provoking and its setting far
grander. But it is weak just where *Sinful Davey* was strong—in its
central roles. Instead of the exuberant John Hurt and the beguiling
Robert Morley, both impeccably professional actors, there are two
awkward teenagers, unsure of what to do either with each other or for
the camera.

The source was a book of the same title by Hans Koningsberger, who
insured the film's fidelity to his book by doing the script himself. Book
and film tell a tale of young lovers swept up in the chaos and bloodshed
of a peasants' uprising in France in 1358. The novel's style is one of
rigorous simplicity, told through the eyes of its protagonist, a student
who leaves the sanctuary of Paris with the intention of crossing the
channel to continue his studies at Oxford. On the way he meets a lovely noblewoman; they fall in love and together face a world in turmoil
where human life seems to have lost all value. The landscape's natural
beauty is lyrically described and contrasted with the horrors men per-
petuate on each other. In defiance of those horrors, the young lovers
pursue their private joys, realizing that their only weapon against the
suffering and death around them is to savor the few moments of hap-
piness allowed them before they too are consumed by the reigning
madness.

The challenge the tale posed to Huston was in a way the antithesis
of that of *Reflections in a Golden Eye*. In the earlier film, the goal had
been to make credible very peculiar individuals in the most banal of
settings. The problem now was to make believable a very alien setting,

a far distant age, yet whose characters were personifications of any pair of lovers anywhere. The tale demanded the evocation of a world as fantastic as McCullers's army base had been ordinary, peopled by two personalities as ordinary as Brando and Harris had been fantastic. Huston succeeded at both.

The settings of *A Walk with Love and Death* are lovely to behold. Huston had planned to re-create medieval France amid the actual remaining traces of it, but the unrest that shook the country in May 1968 forced shooting to be relocated in Austria. The change in no way detracted from the evocation, however; the misty forests, romantic castles, candle-lit banquet halls, magnificent cloudscapes, green meadows, church interiors illuminated by sun streaming through stained glass, are enchanting. The spectacle of warfare has none of the grubby veracity of *The Red Badge of Courage;* it, too, seems to have the quality of a manuscript illumination brought to life. There is a chanting procession of black knights, the charge of warriors in suits of armor spurring their horses across a hillside, a pitched battle between mounted knights and ragged peasants. As a colorful tapestry of a distant romantic past, the film is without fault.

At the dramatic center of the tapestry, however, are two inexperienced performers with a number of faults. As the tale's heroine, Huston cast his daughter Anjelica; as its hero, Assaf Dayan, son of the Israeli defense minister. Both are pleasant to look at, but the former seems traumatized by fear of paternal disapproval and the latter by the cruelties imposed by the English language upon those who are just learning to speak it. Huston had succeeded in making his protagonists ordinary enough to represent young lovers everywhere, but at too high a price. They do not ruin the pleasures to be had from his lyrical dream of medieval life, but they diminish them.

The Kremlin Letter (1970)

Ever true to his practice of never making the same mistake twice, Huston moved quickly on to an entirely different enterprise and, little more than four months after the release of *A Walk with Love and Death* (to tepid critical and popular response), *The Kremlin Letter* was in theaters. Again, its faults and virtues seemed almost deliberately to contrast with what had preceded it. The wide-eyed innocence of Anjelica Huston and Assaf Dayan was followed by the hard experience of such veteran actors as Richard Boone, Patrick O'Neal, and George Sanders. The earlier film had treated sex as a poetic celebration of life; its successor, as a cynical escape from it. The only remote link between the two works was their high technical quality.

The Kremlin Letter is a spy thriller, a genre that Huston had paro-

died in *Across the Pacific* and *Beat the Devil* but had never treated
seriously. The huge popularity of the series of James Bond adventures
starring Sean Connery (*Casino Royale* was not among them) had set
off a flurry of secret agent movies in the sixties. The Bond films, which
began with *Dr. No* in 1963, made clear-cut distinctions between their
heroes and villains. But just two years later, director Martin Ritt
brought a story by John LeCarré to the screen that suggested that in
real intelligence work the good guys and the bad guys were hard to
tell apart. *The Spy Who Came in from the Cold* (1965) presented Richard Burton as a worn-out agent tired of the amorality on both sides in
the Cold War. By the time Huston entered the field, the us-against-
them patriotic spy movie was still alive (Hitchcock gave such a story
exemplary treatment in *Topaz*, released just a few weeks earlier), but
the both-sides-are-corrupt variant was no longer a novelty. The message of *The Kremlin Letter* that everybody in the Cold War was reduced to ruthless cynicism by the duties required of them did not need
reiteration.

"In this film nobody has a single moral, ethical principle," Huston
told an interviewer with what seemed like pride, pointing out that he
felt the story was a "reflection of the moral climate of our times."[3] He
and assistant Gladys Hill had written the screenplay from a novel by
Noel Behn apparently with the idea that the portrayal of a dissolute
moral climate allowed a dissolution of narrative clarity. The characters'
casual unscrupulousness is matched by an even more casual attitude
toward keeping the plot line comprehensible. The confusion does not
have the joyfulness of *Beat the Devil*, where the viewer is soon assured
that trying to keep the story's loose ends tied up is unnecessary (as
well as impossible). The disorder is frustrating because the mood is so
serious and the issues involved purportedly ones of global importance.
And so up to the very end, the viewer keeps wearily trying to sort
things out. The pity is that the effort to untangle the plot leaves little
time to appreciate the work's fragmented virtues.

There is, for example, the sheer spectacle of the locations: a wintry
Helsinki standing in as Moscow, Huston's own preferred retreat and
site of *The Night of the Iguana*, the west coast of Mexico, and some
scenes on the streets of New York City. There is the work of interesting
actors: grizzled Richard Boone as a savagely skillful agent looking out
only for himself, Patrick O'Neal as a dedicated naval officer pulled
down into the murky depths of espionage against his will, Max von
Sydow as a bloodlessly disciplined Soviet agent, Orson Welles as his
cunning Kremlin superior, George Sanders as an operative working
under the cover of transvestism and, most provocative of all, Bibi Andersson as von Sydow's unfaithful wife. Disgusted with her husband's
unsavory profession, Andersson seeks solace through sexual abandon

and, in a startling reversal of movie cliché, hires O'Neal, who is posing as a male prostitute, to amuse her. What begins as a purely carnal desire becomes a deeper need for Andersson after a number of passionate encounters and she, alone of all the film's characters, becomes genuinely sympathetic—erotic and sincere. It is a magnetic performance and had she figured more prominently in the story, she might have given it some emotional gravity. But she enters it after so many villains and convoluted plot twists that it is beyond rehabilitation. The whole of *The Kremlin Letter* does not do justice to the strength of many of its parts.

It looked at first as if Huston was to move from one unfeelingly violent film to another: he agreed to direct George C. Scott in a story about an over-the-hill driver for the Mafia who takes on one more job for pride's sake. *The Last Run* (1971) turned out to be Scott's way of telling the world how attractive he was to young women (he seduces its heroine), and Huston fortunately realized that the actor was in control soon enough to bow out. It was finished by the competent journeyman director Richard Fleischer. Still, the fact that Huston had consented to work with what was clearly a mediocre script was an ominous sign. As he entered his sixty-fifth year, it increasingly seemed that he, like the man who replaced him on *The Last Run*, was content to be an anonymous craftsman whose fortunes rose and fell with the scripts that happened to land in his lap.

Two decades after James Agee had written that he was "the most inventive director of his generation" and that he had "done more to extend, invigorate, and purify the essential idiom of American movies, the truly visual telling of stories, than anyone since the prime of D. W. Griffith,"[4] most critics considered Huston a has-been. Since roughly the time of *The Barbarian and the Geisha*, reviewers had taken to lamenting Huston's decline. But if Agee had, as Andrew Sarris claimed, "canonized Huston prematurely,"[5] the artistic obituaries were just as premature. It was true that Huston appeared to be taking on work indiscriminately, but as *Reflections in a Golden Eye* proved, if somehow he found himself with great material, the results might be no less so. In 1972, that is just what occured.

More than anyone, producer Ray Stark was in a position to realize that while indifferent material was likely to result in an indifferent Huston film, good material tended to produce good Huston films. When Stark had given him Tennessee Williams's *The Night of the Iguana*, the director had made of it a film no worse than the play. When he had given him McCullers's *Reflections in a Golden Eye*, he received a film worthy of a very fine book. Now he gave him a beautifully observed low-key meditation on the lives of people on the lower fringe of the professional boxing world, a novel called *Fat City* by

Leonard Gardner, and Huston made one of the finest, most personal works of his career.

Fat City (1972)

Huston's adaptation from Gardner is in a way more moving than his earlier ones from Hammett, Crane, Melville, and McCullers, not because his source was superior but because it was closer to his own life. He had never been a private eye in San Francisco, a deserter in the Civil War, a Nantucket sea captain, or a repressed homosexual army captain, but he had been a boxer. When Huston went back to southern California twenty years after shooting his last film there, he returned to a scene of an important chapter in his childhood, a chapter that, as the director of *Freud* would likely to have been the first to admit, had a formative influence on his adult life.

As a young boy Huston had been treated as an invalid by his mother, and he had rebelled violently against it. Boxing had been a major part of his effort to assert his vitality. "When I stopped being 'an invalid,' why, physical things attracted me very much and I discovered that I had a kind of talent for boxing," he later reminisced.

I began boxing in high school, and then I went to a school called Lincoln Heights. There were two future world's champions going to the school at the time. It was in a seedy part of Los Angeles. . . . Then there were little clubs around the city and boxing at them all was an adventure for me. I enjoyed the atmosphere, there were great chums and good friends. . . . When I put on gloves, I felt easy and I hit straight. I was so damned skinny I'd feel a beating for several days afterwards. I had in mind to become middleweight champion of the world! I had a few more fights. I was very lucky and pretty good. It wasn't a lonely life, it was a very full life, very full, crammed full.[6]

The protagonists of *Fat City* are neither very lucky nor pretty good, and their lives are not very full. But boxing holds out the hope of changing all that, the only hope. Huston had other doors open to him besides boxing and he realized they held more promise and less risk than striving to be middleweight champion of the world. But he knew and understood those who had no other means of changing their lot in life. When he brought them to the screen, it was with unmistakable exactitude and empathy. They were miserable, pathetic figures, but Huston treated them without a trace of condescension. Instead there is a quality of deep admiration for the people who, as he described them, "have the heroism to go on taking it on the chin in life as well as in the ring."[7]

The first thing that seems different from and more intense than previous Huston films is *Fat City*'s sense of place. Shot in a run-down section of Stockton, California, made up of, in Huston's words, "crummy little hotels; gaps between buildings like missing teeth; people— blacks and whites—standing around or sitting on orange crates; little gambling halls where they played for nickels and dimes" (*OB*, 339), the film recorded an area that was razed not long afterward. It has a certain exoticism in the sense of its being alien to the average moviegoer, but it is not the glamorous exoticism of most Huston settings— Africa, Tobago, Mexico, Austria, or the rolling hills of Ireland. It is not, in short, a place that American viewers would dream of deliberately visiting themselves, but a place like the ones they close their eyes to if obliged to pass through them in the course of everyday life. Huston had put such a place on the screen only once before, in one of his best films, *The Asphalt Jungle*. That film, though, had portrayed the dark side of American city life as evoked by the MGM art department. This time Huston and his cinematographer, Conrad Hall, were out in the unmanicured real world, recording the way the relentless California sun beat down on buildings and streets that were the home of people battered by poverty and alcohol. How, an interviewer asked Huston when *Fat City* was released, could such a cosmopolitan gentleman who had been living regally all over the world suddenly return to a place he had not been in twenty years and capture its spirit so well? "Maybe," replied Huston, "I have a little perspective on it."[8]

Everywhere present in the films is that sense of perspective on the "great chums and good friends" he had made in "a seedy part of Los Angeles" and gained in the many years spent so far from them. Yet the film's impact owes just as much to three actors who belonged to a generation not even born when Huston was pursuing his boxing career: Stacy Keach, Jeff Bridges, and Susan Tyrell, playing respectively an ex-boxer down on his luck and dreaming unrealistically of a comeback, an aspiring younger fighter who seems perfectly positioned to make the same mistakes as his older friend, and an alcoholic woman with the gift of making even the simplest statement seem wildly ill thought out. The trio form a ceaselessly engaging ensemble. The lot of these characters is not outwardly a funny one, but the quality of Gardner's script, Huston's direction, and their own superb acting make their plight as strangely comic as it is sad. In the boozy exchanges between Keach and Tyrell in grubby barrooms, and in awkward discussions between Bridges and his girlfriend, wonderfully played by Candy Clark, on the subjects of sex and marriage, there is a tone that is extraordinary precisely because of the way it captures the ordinary.

There is the smell and texture of drab afternoons in shabby hotel rooms, the predawn air of broad fields of onions as groggy day laborers tumble out of old buses to begin a day of back-breaking work, and all-night diners whose patrons have one foot in the grave. But the most intense smells and textures of *Fat City* are those Huston could still recall after knowing them at firsthand a half-century earlier: the combination of sweat, cigar smoke, blinding lights, and deafening crowds that was a boxing match; the atmosphere of the dressing room where a would-be Muhammad Ali tries to boost his own morale ("Ya gotta wanna kick ass"), the blare of the loudspeakers announcing "Irish Ernie Munger" ("But I'm not Irish," says Munger; "I just put it that way so they know you're white," says his manager), the bone-crushing violence of the ring, followed by hurried intervals between bouts ("They're all bloody," complains Munger's successor when given his trunks to wear; "Don't worry about it," says the manager, "it's not your blood"). Then comes the bruised aftermath in a gaudy barroom over beers: "We'll fix up that nose," says the ever-ebullient manager, "Look at mine, wouldya believe it had ever been broke?" "Yes," replies the wounded fighter.

Fat City is a film too rich in detail to be absorbed in a single viewing, and too rich in characters to make one want to part company with them after only a brief ninety minutes. The viewer is drawn back in the hopes of resolving an apparent paradox: why is it that such unfortunate, unglamorous people, whose lives seem so wasted, hold such fascination? The answer lies perhaps partly in the loving detail in which their world is portrayed, partly in the pleasure of watching some of the best talents of a new generation of performers, partly in wisely colloquial dialogue and deftly staged dramatic confrontations. But the final reason that *Fat City* is a Huston masterpiece may be the strangely noble sense of heroism it communicates, "the heroism to go on taking it on the chin in life as well as in the ring."

12

Wise Blood

ALWAYS DEPENDENT ON the quality of his scripts and ever erratic in his choice of them, Huston moved from the low-key, gently observant world of Leonard Gardner to the bombastic, crudely caricatured one of John Milius. Full of enthusiasm for graphic violence, bathroom humor, and misogyny, *The Life and Times of Judge Roy Bean* (1972) appears to deliberately repudiate the virtues of *Fat City*. Where the former quietly studied the textures of real life, the latter exults in comic strip exaggeration; where the former treated conventionally unappealing characters with sympathy, the latter takes conventionally appealing ones and makes them unpleasant. The carefully modulated rhythms of Huston's previous film made its ninety minutes seem too short; the ragged edges and lurching pace of its successor make its two hours seem interminable. Once again Huston demonstrated his capacity for lowering himself to the level of his material.

The Mackintosh Man (1973)

If *Judge Roy Bean* had been in any way characteristic of Huston's work, he would deserve to be taken to task for it, to be blamed for its pointless brutality and misanthropy. But it, as much as anything he had ever done, has everything to do with its writer and virtually nothing to do with its director. Huston's philosophy was clearly to avoid inactivity at any price and he admitted as much in explaining how he came to make his next film, *The Mackintosh Man*: "I'm always working or occupied. In fact, I don't think making pictures is work, any more than a painter thinks he's at work. It's what I *do*. . . . Having finished 'The Judge,' I had nothing to go into immediately, nor did Paul Newman or John Foreman, the producer, or the whole group who worked on 'The Judge,' and I think it was a reluctance to separate. Here was the opportunity to go on and do another film and have a good time!"[1]

Such an introduction would seem to warn off anyone unamused by the gory horseplay of Huston's previous project, but the one member of the crew who did not stick around was the one whose personality

'wo faces of Paul Newman: (top) The Life and Times of 127
udge Roy Bean; (bottom) The Mackintosh Man. *Courtesy*
f the Museum of Modern Art, Film Stills Archive.

had been as influential as Huston's was absent, John Milius. "I don't seek to interpret reality by placing my stamp on it," Huston reminded an interviewer during the production of *The Mackintosh Man*. "I try to be as faithful as I can to the material I have chosen to film. Everything technical and artistic in the picture is designed to depict that material for an audience."[2] This time the material was a spy thriller by Desmond Morris, adapted by Walter Hill, and it was as different from Milius's work as it was from Melville's, McCullers's, or Gardner's. And Huston was back in Ireland working with cinematographer Oswald Morris. There was nothing highly distinctive about the overall result, but there was at least that most reliable virtue of Huston films: an attractive variety of settings.

Across the Pacific and *Beat the Devil* had proved that Huston could poke wonderful fun at the spy thriller genre, but *The Kremlin Letter* had indicated that he was not particularly adept at taking it seriously. Unfortunately, *The Mackintosh Man* was no parody. Again the cast contained gifted actors, Paul Newman and James Mason, but again the story became too muddled to sustain real suspense and was outshown by the scenery behind it. Newman played an Australian spy, but soon forgot to use an Australian accent. The female lead, French actress Dominique Sanda, played an Englishwoman though her English was as bad as Assaf Dayan's in *A Walk with Love and Death*. The fact that some of her lines were so awkwardly pronounced as to be unintelligible became still another handicap for a film suffering from a none-too-clear plot.

The Mackintosh Man is not as coldbloodedly cynical as *The Kremlin Letter*, but neither is it much more absorbing. Like its predecessor, it seems to beg for the expertise of Alfred Hitchcock. The minor pleasures it offers all lie in its picturesque locales and a couple of well-executed action sequences. Among the former are some nice shots of London and the island of Malta and a celebration of the director's beloved countryside and seacoast in Ireland. There is a striking chase across some brooding moors with a burning manor house in the background and a Gaelic cross outlined against a cold, gray sky. And a rousing high-speed car chase is staged along a stunning stretch of coastline with Newman at the wheel of a dashing white Mercedes with villains pursuing him in a large truck. In Malta, another short surge of excitement is provided by an underwater sequence in which the intrepid Newman dons diving gear to best his foes. After the unpleasantness of *Judge Roy Bean*, these simple pleasures are welcome in a Huston film, but they do little to suggest that he was capable of much more and about to prove it.

Two decades earlier, as he was completing *Moby Dick*, Huston decided he had already waited too long to bring a work by one of his favorite writers, Rudyard Kipling, to the screen. Three years earlier, basking in the success of *The African Queen*, a tale of heroics in a remote corner of the British Empire, he had discussed tackling a similar theme with screenwriter Peter Viertel: an adaptation of Kipling's *The Man Who Would Be King*. Other projects had intervened but with Melville's nineteenth-century adventure classic just finished, the time seemed right for one of Kipling's. Huston arranged for producer Walter Mirisch to purchase the rights from the Kipling estate and set out to scout locations in India. But *Moby Dick* did not become the financial success it was expected to be and the backing for another big-scale epic dissolved. Huston retreated to the simplicity of *Heaven Knows, Mr. Allison*. Still, the dream of immersing himself in the world of the author he had adored in his boyhood lived on. During the shooting of *The Misfits*, Clark Gable refired the director's enthusiasm by expressing his own for playing the lead role. It had been Huston's original idea to pair Gable with Bogart but soon afterward Bogart died. Then no sooner was Huston moved by Gable's interest to find a replacement for Bogart than news of Gable's death reached him. As the years passed and he moved from one disparate project to another, Huston accumulated no less than three scripts for the Kipling story as well as a portfolio of sketches for the project by Stephen Grimes. Finally in 1973, in what Huston described as "our mutual guilt following *The Mackintosh Man*," he, John Foreman, and Paul Newman decided to take on the story because, in contrast to their last two films, "it would be something we could hold our heads up about afterward" (*OB*, 351). Newman and Robert Redford were to fill the shoes vacated by Bogart and Gable.

Newman, however, showing a critical acumen that apparently had deserted him when he had chosen to work on Huston's two previous films, contended that he and Redford were less appropriate choices than two real Englishmen would be and he went on to name the two he thought ideal: Sean Connery and Michael Caine. Huston heartily agreed, as did the two British actors. Putting together the financing for the five-million-dollar production proved more troublesome than the casting, however, and for two years the project remained in limbo.

The Man Who Would Be King (1975)

Locations were scouted in several remote corners of the globe since the actual setting of the story, Kafiristan, was as closed to foreigners as it had been in Kipling's day. Other Himalayan regions posed too many logistical problems; Turkey seemed promising until political problems ruled it out. Finally, Stephen Grimes's proposal of the Atlas Mountains in Morocco was accepted. This time delays, financial obstructions, and casting problems failed to derail the project. Connery and Caine kept themselves available, John Foreman managed to strike a deal with a variety of backers and, by the beginning of 1975, Huston was in Morocco with his actors, a script he and Gladys Hill had distilled from the earlier versions, his preferred cameraman, Oswald Morris, the great art director Alexander Trauner, and extras who reportedly numbered fifteen thousand. His long-delayed homage to Rudyard Kipling was finally ready to roll.

The appeal of *The Man Who Would Be King* lies in part in its being simultaneously very modern and very old-fashioned. It is modern in the sense that it pays a documentarylike attention to an exotic world— scorpion swallowers, snake charmers, and other strange beings amid a teeming urban marketplace, eerie nocturnal desert landscapes with snow-capped mountains in the background. The authenticity of place caught by highly mobile cameras shooting in color for the wide screen give the film the look of the seventies production that it is.

But in spirit it makes absolutely no concessions to the era in which it was made, maintaining an absolute loyalty to both Kipling's view of things and the earlier age of Hollywood adventure movies Kipling helped inspire, such as George Stevens's *Gunga Din* (1939). Huston makes no effort to impose a veneer of latter-day social consciousness on the story by toning down the racism and imperialism implicit in the idea of two Britons establishing themselves as rulers over non-Western peoples. A fashionable bow to third world politics would have been alien to Rudyard Kipling and infidelity to a classic literary source was one artistic sin of which Huston could never have been accused. The work has the unself-conscious rambunctiousness of the teenage boy Huston must have been when he fell in love with the story for the first time. It is clear and straightforward with its heroes and villains distinctly defined; not a trace remains of the muddled convolutions of Huston's contemporary-era thrillers, *The Kremlin Letter* and *The Mackintosh Man*.

The simplicity of the story is only exceeded by the grandeur of the spectacle. Morris's camera and Trauner's designs combine to create a series of breathtaking tableaux. A rainbow of multicolored turbans passes by, as their wearers cling to the roof of an overloaded train chugging across a vast plain. A fierce blizzard high in a mountain pass traps the heroes until a gigantic avalanche fills the precipitous crevice that blocked their way. There are massed cavalry charges down broad mountainsides, the pageant of thousands of warriors about to attack each other suddenly falling prostrate before a passing holy man, fantastic waterfalls, and bizarre mountaintop temples.

The story is in some ways a retelling of that of *Sierra Madre* and those observers who still had the courage to try to find consistent themes in Huston's work were quick to point out that the Kipling tale was a failed quest in the tradition of *Sierra Madre*, *We Were Strangers*, *The Asphalt Jungle*, and *Moby Dick*. Once again the principal characters are hopeless eccentrics with a crazy ambition who, against all odds, come to realize their goal only to see it slip away as easily as the struggle to attain it had been hard. But a crucial difference is the absence of bitter irony; this time the excitement of the quest is forthrightly presented as having been worth its price. The death of Connery's character, Daniel Dravot, becomes not so much a cruel joke played on him by "the Lord, fate, nature or whatever you prefer," but simply the toll he more or less willingly paid to achieve his goal.

The comparison with *Sierra Madre*, in fact, can be quite misleading. It is true that both stories follow men into wild territory where the lure of untold riches enchants them and that in the end they find those riches but are, because of a weakness in their own characters, unable to return to the civilized world with them. But as their respective titles suggest, the actual goals pursued are quite unalike: the aim of the prospectors in the 1948 film was treasure, that of the adventurers of almost three decades later was for one of them to be a king. Caine's character, Peachy Carnehan, points out to Dravot that the opportunity is theirs to "fill our pockets and walk out of here millionaires, the two richest men in England, in the world." But Dravot's thoughts are elsewhere: he has become a king, now why not a god? With a gold crown on his head and cheering masses by the thousands prostrate before him, he has fulfilled his original ambition but has developed a new one.

Carnehan thinks they have had "a rare streak of luck" but Dravot knows better: "You call it luck, I call it destiny." Carried away by his power, Dravot insists on taking a wife, though his partner and all the omens are against it. His wife proves him mortal and the revelation of his mortality brings his downfall. And his fall from grace is literal—he tumbles from a rope bridge into a seemingly bottomless ravine and, as Carnehan recalls that "it took him half an hour to fall," a haunting shot shows him disappearing into the abyss. But Dravot had become, if only for a while, exactly what he had wanted to become, a king. *The Man Who Would Be King* is not a failed quest at all; it is a gloriously exciting successful one. And it was also a rousing confirmation that, when impassioned by his material, the director whom critics had long taken to dismissing as having "nothing in reserve to even faintly remind us of the skill that made such classics" had still everything it took to make another classic.

A close follower of Huston's career might have been excused a sense of gloomy foreboding right after the release of *The Man Who Would Be King* precisely because of its triumphant success. For almost two decades Huston had never moved from one complete artistic success

Daniel Dravot (Sean Connery), having achieved his ambition in The Man Who
Would Be King, *is about to overreach himself while Peachy Carnehan (Michael
Caine) looks on skeptically. Courtesy of the Museum of Modern Art, Film Stills
Archive.*

to another. But, for reasons no more explicable than those that led him
to make a series of mediocre films, he now followed his Kipling adventure with two small-scale projects that worked just as well on their
own, considerably different, terms. The first was a departure not just
in subject and scale, but in format: not since *Let There Be Light* had
Huston made a film shorter than feature length or intended for other
than theatrical release. *Independence* (1975) runs a brisk twenty-eight
minutes and was commissioned by the National Park Service to be
shown in Independence Hall in Philadelphia as part of the observation
of the bicentennial of American independence.

Independence (1975)

"I was asked," he recalled, "how it felt to be making a 'small film'
after making 'big pictures,' but really I don't know the difference between a major or a minor film. The fact that the narrative takes half an

hour to tell doesn't change my thinking or my effort. If the film conveys a strong and meaningful message, then I'm quite satisfied that it's a major film."[3] The skill at establishing mood and atmosphere, and the finesse with actors that Huston brought to *Independence* is in no way inferior to its lavish predecessor.

The film is set at Independence Hall itself, the meeting place for the founders of the American republic. First to appear is Benjamin Franklin, likably incarnated by Eli Wallach. Franklin is granted the wish he supposedly made at the end of his life to see the country after two centuries, and in exchange he takes the modern viewer back to the formative days of the new republic. "I'm sixty-eight," he exults, "How excellent it is to be young again!" (Huston himself had just turned sixty-nine.) Franklin is soon joined by such illustrious contemporaries as John Adams (Pat Hingle), Thomas Jefferson (Ken Howard), and George Washington (Patrick O'Neal), and, one by one, they offer their commentaries on the times when "independence" was still "the word they dare not whisper." The men speak of "a breach that can never be healed," "a government of laws not of men," and tell the late twentieth-century American that "you have a republic if you can keep it."

There is not a lot of dramatic action in *Independence;* its impact, except for a few shots Huston obviously could not resist of horses dashing through sylvan glens relaying messages to the Continental Congress, comes from the elocutionary power of its actors. Sometimes they are gathered on a foggy lawn or are alone in a candle-lit study, but most often they speak from Independence Hall itself. The direct expository style of treating historical ideas has strong similarities to the last films of the great Italian filmmaker Roberto Rossellini who, at the end of his career, abandoned fictional dramas altogether to explore the lives and thoughts of such figures as Socrates, Lorenzo de' Medici, and Louis XIV. Like Rossellini's work, Huston's condescends to neither his subject nor his audience, presents complex ideas simply yet without oversimplifying, and manages to make involving cinema out of a subject that seemed inherently uncinematic. The spirit of patriotism is genuine and appealing; the wayward international filmmaker paid sincere tribute to the democratic traditions of his native land.

With the twin achievements of the epic *The Man Who Would Be King* and the unassuming *Independence* just behind him, Huston had set the stage for a most honorable retirement. And when he was hospitalized for major heart surgery on his over seventy-year-old body, it seemed that retirement was about to be enforced. But Huston bounced back physically just as he had always done artistically and proclaimed his intention never to slow down: "I have had a lot of fun making films. The time to quit is when it is no longer fun. I can't see that happening soon."[4] On another occasion he stated, "I love my work. Each film is a little life that grows and is nurtured by some people who will probably never be together again. You go from beginning to end together and when you are done and you go away, there is a certain sadness."[5] The only remedy for that sadness, Huston implied, was to start another "little life" as soon as possible. In January 1979, his health restored, he was in Macon, Georgia, doing just that.

Wise Blood (1979)

Wise Blood could have been proclaimed a brilliant repudiation of the outmoded traditions of the commercial film industry if it had not been made by someone who had worked steadily within that industry for close to half a century. It had the hallmarks of the work of a rebellious young director contemptuous of big budgets, overpaid stars, and easy-to-digest stories that offended no one. It was shot by a close-knit group of family and friends working for very little pay in a remote unglamorous Southern town. Its actors had talent but little celebrity; its story held fascination but little spectacle.

Like the best Huston works before it, Wise Blood's strength came from its source, a short novel by Flannery O'Connor, her first, published in 1952. The book is a bizarre and often hilarious portrait of religious fanaticism in the Deep South. O'Connor wrote about the world she lived in and her description of the book's subject puts it best: "The religion of the South is a do-it-yourself religion, something which I, as a Catholic, find painful and touching and grimly comic. It's full of unconscious pride that lands them in all sorts of ridiculous religious predicaments. They have nothing to correct their practical heresies and so they work them out dramatically."[6] The story follows a rural boy raised by a fanatical evangelist grandfather (Huston created a cameo role for the character and played it himself). Upon his discharge from the army at the end of World War II, the boy, Hazel Motes, sets out for his region's largest city "to do some things I never have done before." He thinks his intention is to escape the evangelistic fever in his blood, but no escape is possible; his "unconscious pride" only leads him into deeper and more grotesque "ridiculous religious predicaments." O'Connor's gift lay in part in her ability to render those predicaments both credible and "painful and touching and grimly comic." The world she creates has such inner consistency that, although Hazel Mote's eccentricity barely surpasses that of almost everyone he stumbles into contact with, all her characters are both real and inexplicably sympathetic.

When a young man, Michael Fitzgerald, who had acquired the rights to O'Connor's story, set out to find a director, he had good reason to approach Huston. And Huston, though he surely could have found more lucrative work, must have seen in the demented world of *Wise Blood* an atmosphere just right for creating another "little life." Fitzgerald was no stereotypical producer out for a profit. His father, eminent poet and translator Robert Fitzgerald, was O'Connor's literary executor; his mother had edited her collected letters. O'Connor had actually written the novel while staying with the Fitzgeralds. Michael's brother Benedict turned the work into a screenplay while he, after securing Huston's promise to direct, embarked on a long, disheartening search for backing. Other than Huston's erratic track record, he did not have much to sell; he had never produced a film before and O'Connor's work had never been successfully adapted for one. The money he finally found—from some Germans who arranged for the advance sale of European distribution and television rights—was a pittance by American film industry standards, less than two million dollars. But Huston, the Fitzgeralds, and a terrific cast were supplied with a commodity better than money when they assembled in Macon, Georgia: a love for their work.

From *The Maltese Falcon* through *Reflections in a Golden Eye* and *Fat City*, the literary source of Huston's best films often seemed drawn from the screen rather than the reverse, so uncannily well did he find actors to fit their characters. *Wise Blood* became another such instance. The faultless casting included Brad Dourif as Hazel Motes, Daniel Shor as his near-moronic sidekick, Amy Wright as a salacious teenager, Harry Dean Stanton as her irascible preacher-huckster father, and Ned Beatty as a money-hungry promoter of evangelism. Though most of the cast were barely born when the book was written, there remains the impression that just as Hammett seemed to have created Sam Spade for Bogart, O'Connor had written with them in mind.

Using an innovative camera device that permitted the camera operator to follow his subject on foot while maintaining a steady shot, Huston tracked along the streets of Macon catching the effect of dull winter sunlight on the drab streets and faded billboards. As the ravaged or half-crazed faces of his characters interact against the banal backdrop, the atmosphere is somehow both depressed and turbulent. Every human confrontation seems to be between beings who are at once subnormal in intelligence and exceptional in their psychic energy, their "wise blood." And in the mixture of stupidity and spirituality lies the grim comedy.

When a cabdriver seeks to explain to himself why Hazel Motes, who he is sure is a preacher, is going to visit a prostitute, he concludes logically that "you can tell people more about sin if you know it first hand." "I ain't no preacher," Motes protests to the whore. "Mama don't mind if you ain't no preacher," she replies, "so long as you got four dollars." Motes finally concedes that he is a preacher but not for Jesus, for "Jesus is a trick on niggers." He represents the "Church of Truth Without Christ." "Is that something foreign?" asks his prospective landlady. "Oh no ma'am," Motes assures her, "Protestant." Motes's religion extends to the automotive world: "Nobody with a good car needs to be justified" and "Nobody with a good car needs to worry about nothing." The decrepit car in question, as well as the weary sharp-edged faces it lurches past and the desolate landscape behind them, turns his feeble wisdom into pathos.

Wise Blood works in many of the same curious ways as Fat City. Everybody in both films is a loser, playing out his life in disheartening surroundings, yet the viewer's interest in them never flags. Their peculiarities, however repellent, are never boring; their plight, however pathetic, never stops exciting one's curiosity. And the contradiction can be explained in some of the same ways: attention to detail, acting talent, engaging dialogue, and adroit staging. But O'Connor's world is darker and more deranged than Gardner's, and Huston's adaptation reflects the difference. There is less underlying empathy for these religious obsessives in Georgia than for the inhabitants of Stockton's skid row. Some viewers may thus share the feelings of critic Andrew Sarris, who stated that "I respect the film enormously, but I don't have the slightest desire ever to see it again." Sarris added that "every thoughtful person should see Wise Blood once if only to experience a profound and original depression."[7] But as grim as the story ultimately is, its grimness never defeats its comedy, which, in some instances, such as an encounter between Shor and a gorilla suit, is actually quite light-hearted. And one could also argue that the effect of watching the convergence of a very fine director with gifted performers and compelling material is just the opposite of depression even if the message is not cheerful.

Exhilaration may be a strange word to use in relation to a story about ignorant and unbalanced people, but it is an appropriate one to describe the effect of seeing Huston return to the top of his form. When Hazel Motes's landlady discovers that he has bound himself with barbed wire in penance for his sins, she patiently explains to him that it's something people have quit doing—"like boiling in oil or being a saint or walling up cats. There's no reason for it. People have quit doing it." Motes's response is simple and unanswerable: "They ain't quit doing it as long as I'm doing it." One imagines someone telling Huston that forty-year veterans of the golden age of Hollywood have quit making lively, unorthodox movies just for the love of it. Since their place in film history has already been determined and their fortunes assured, there's no reason for it, so they've quit doing it. And then one sees Huston's wrinkled face smiling gently and replying: "They ain't quit doing it as long as I'm doing it."

After *Wise Blood,* as he had after *Reflections in a Golden Eye* and *Fat City* Huston retreated from the challenge of making wonderful movies from wonderful books and drifted through unexceptional projects. After the better part of half a century in the film business, inconsistency remained the great constant of his career—that and an aversion to inactivity.

Phobia (1980), made in Canada and never theatrically released in the United States, is a competently manufactured murder mystery, a production about which Huston could not have felt strongly. He admitted as much in an on-the-set interview when asked about his favorite film: "You always believe your current one is the best, although I wouldn't say that in this instance."[8] Nor is there much evidence of real passion in *Victory* (1981), which was shot in Hungary and combines the clichés of both sports and prisoner-of-war movies. Like its predecessor, it can charitably be described as professionally executed and easy to forget. Far more fanfare surrounded Huston's adaptation of the stage musical *Annie* (1981), but traces of its director's personality were as minuscule as its budget was gigantic.

Where such a string of uninteresting works had in previous decades provoked critical aspersion, reaction now tended toward condescending wonder that the old man could still climb into a director's chair. The eulogistic respect was typified by the bestowal of the American Film Institute's Life Achievement Award, which, in the case of such Huston colleagues as John Ford, Alfred Hitchcock, and Frank Capra, had served as unofficial acknowledgment that their working lives were over. Yet, with typical Huston contrariness, the AFI obsequies became a catalyst for another adventure.

Huston had invited to the ceremonial dinner a diverse group of men who together would enable him to bring Malcolm Lowry's novel *Under the Volcano* to the screen. They were two German producers, Wieland Schulz-Keil and Moritz Borman, who were near the end of an exhausting effort to secure the rights for the novel from the Lowry estate; Michael Fitzgerald, whose determination to bring about the filming of *Wise Blood* had had such happy results; and Alberto Isaac from the Mexican Cinematographic Institute. While his admirers praised him as if he had retired and his detractors murmured that Huston would lazily lend his name to any movie if the money was good, plans were hatched for a difficult project to be shot on a budget so low no one involved would collect his customary salary.

Like another film a long time in the offing, *The Man Who Would Be*

The dramatic rescue of Orphan Annie after the climactic chase sequence in Annie.
Courtesy of Movie Star News.

King, Under the Volcano had been talked of as a Huston film many
times before, if not so much by Huston himself as by others who had
dreamed of a marriage between a book about dying in Mexico and a
director who had chosen to live there. Lowry wrote his story about a
man's war with himself in Mexico in the late thirties, about the time
Huston was working on the script of *Juarez,* dealing with another sort
of Mexican war. After several reworkings, the book was finally published in 1947, at the time Huston was shooting his fable of self-de-
struction in the Sierra Madre. Little wonder then that treatments of
Lowry's work pursued Huston everywhere his erratic career took him.
When first contacted by producer Schulz-Kiel, he reportedly answered wearily, "I've heard about this project 150 times. Why not
151?"[9]
     If Huston lacked the enthusiasm that had sustained him in his long
wait to film Rudyard Kipling's story, it was because he had never
shared the widespread conviction that the book was a natural for the
screen. "It's not an easy book," he pointed out with considerable un-
derstatement, "its excellence is literary. . . . There's an awful lot to
wade through."[10] Lowry's work has an often impenetrable density, its
complexities of language, symbol, and metaphor, had defeated every

screen adaptation Huston had seen (he estimated having received, unsolicited, at least twenty-five over the years). Its story was even more resistant to visual treatment than the allegorical chapters of *Moby Dick*. Unlike Melville's work, it had very little outward action, taking place almost entirely within the head of a man wracked by suicidal alcoholism.

But the same fortuitous circumstances that had thrown Huston together with the German producers who had been able to navigate the legal maze necessary to get the rights to the novel and the Mexican official willing to lend material and financial support, now turned up a scriptwriter. *Wise Blood* producer Fitzgerald had been looking at samples of the work of a young playwright, Guy Gallo, and had found out that he, like so many others, had tried his hand at a screenplay for *Under the Volcano*. Gallo, however, had realized the necessity of massively simplifying the Lowry work and had pared it down into realizable sequences and a manageable length. Little more than three months after the AFI dinner, Gallo, Fitzgerald, and Schulz-Kiel were at Huston's Mexican home refining a script. Albert Finney (whom Huston had just directed in *Annie*) had signed on for the all-important central role of the Consul, and he was to be supported by Jacqueline Bisset and Anthony Andrews. Soon after, cast and crew—among them Gabriel Figueroa, the cinematographer who had shot some of Luis Bunuel's most incendiary works—were filming in the town where Lowry's story was set, Cuernavaca.

The director of *The Maltese Falcon* was behind the camera again in the summer of 1983 and journalists from around the world came to watch. One of them, Pete Hamill, wrote: "On this day of shooting, he seems to be everywhere, tall, slightly hunched, oddly frail, so bony now that his hands seem immense, like drawings by Egon Schiele. He has had a heart bypass and he wheezes from emphysema. But John Huston is not yet old."[11]

The result was a film that, like its source, fascinates with the reckless, morbid, articulate imagination of its protagonist. But, while respecting Lowry's work, it does not kowtow to it. Where the book becomes convoluted at times to the point of being unreadable, the film has the clarity and luminescence of the Mexican sky. Literature can be absorbed in small doses, but cinema, in most cases, cannot; so Huston found a tone that, unlike Lowry's sometimes repellent prose, progressively entrances. Finney is not just frightening and exasperating, he is also often very funny. The movie's less than two hours may lack some of the richness of Lowry's nearly four hundred dense pages, but it renders its tortured protagonist more human and thus easier to empathize with.

Figueroa's views of Cuernavaca's secret gardens through which the

Consul stumbles, bottle in hand; its streets, churning with the cere-
monies of the Day of the Dead, down which the Consul strolls with
deceptive self-control; and the few ominous glimpses of the volcano
Popocatépetl itself, both seduce and disturb. As Albert Finney rivets
the attention, *Under the Volcano* casts and sustains its spell. Its director was indeed not yet old.

Notes and References

Preface

1. William F. Nolan, *John Huston: King Rebel* (Los Angeles, 1965), 33.
2. Stuart Kaminsky, *John Huston: Maker of Magic* (Boston: Houghton Mifflin, 1978), 14.
3. Axel Madsen, *John Huston* (Garden City, 1978), 36.
4. Gerald Pratley, *The Cinema of John Huston* (New York, 1977), 33.
5. John Huston, *An Open Book* (New York, 1980), 69; hereafter cited in the text as *OB*.

Chapter Two

1. Pratley, *Cinema*, 40.
2. James Agee, *Agee on Film* (New York, 1958), 320.

Chapter Three

1. Agee, *Agee on Film*, 151.

Chapter Four

1. Pratley, *Cinema*, 57.
2. Ibid., 63.
3. B. Traven, *The Treasure of the Sierra Madre* (London: Granada, 1974), 61.
4. Madsen, *Huston*, 80.
5. Kaminsky, *Huston*, 55.
6. Agee, *Agee on Film*, 232.
7. Ibid., 278.

Chapter Five

1. Review of *We Were Strangers*, *Hollywood Reporter*, 27 April 1949.
2. Pratley, *Cinema*, 72.
3. Sterling Hayden, *Wanderer* (New York: Bantam, 1964), 342.
4. Madsen, *Huston*, 101.

5. Quoted in cover publicity of Lillian Ross, *Picture* (New York: Avon, 1969).

6. *Time*, 16 October 1951; *Cue*, 19 October 1951; *Life*, 16 October 1951; *Saturday Review*, 20 October 1951.

7. Ross, *Picture*, 191.

8. *Life*, 16 October 1951.

9. Pratley, *Cinema*, 56.

10. Ross, *Picture*, 177.

Chapter Six

1. *Saturday Review*, 3 March 1952.

2. Agee, *Agee on Film*, 330.

3. Pratley, *Cinema*, 57.

4. Ibid., 94.

5. *New Yorker*, 15 March 1953.

6. Pratley, *Cinema*, 98.

7. Ibid., 99.

8. Ibid., 101.

9. Otis Guernsey, Jr., *New York Herald Tribune*, 13 March 1954; *Time*, 8 March 1954.

10. Nolan, *Huston*, 126.

Chapter Seven

1. Herman Melville, *Moby Dick* (New York: New American Library, 1961), 225.

2. *Time*, 9 July 1956.

3. *Outlook*, 16 August 1930.

4. *Cinema Magazine*, October 1930.

5. Nolan, *Huston*, 132.

6. Oswald Morris, *A New Color for "Moby Dick,"* publicity release for film, 16 April 1956.

7. Pratley, *Cinema*, 106.

8. Nan Robertson, "On the Tumult in Tobago for Mr. Allison," *New York Times*, 15 June 1956.

Chapter Eight

1. Pratley, *Cinema*, 118.

2. Paul P. Kennedy, "Trailing 'The Unforgiven' below the Border," *New York Times*, 1 February 1959.

Chapter Nine

1. Pratley, *Cinema*, 131.

Chapter Ten

1. Pratley, *Cinema*, 140.
2. Madsen, *Huston*, 201.
3. Paul Kennedy, "John Huston's 'Iguana,'" *New York Times*, 1 December 1963.

Chapter Eleven

1. Pratley, *Cinema*, 165.
2. Ibid., 165.
3. Warren Wolf, *Cue*, 28 June 1969, 10.
4. Agee, *Agee on Film*, 330.
5. Andrew Sarris, *The American Cinema* (New York: E. P. Dutton, 1968), 156.
6. Pratley, *Cinema*, 19.
7. Kaminsky, *Huston*, 191.
8. Curtice Taylor and Glenn O'Brien, *Interview*, September 1972, 42.

Chapter Twelve

1. Pratley, *Cinema*, 184.
2. Gene D. Phillips, "Talking with John Huston," *Film Comment*, May 1973.
3. Pratley, *Cinema*, 196.
4. Quoted in Paramount Pictures' publicity release for *Victory*.
5. Andrew H. Malcolm, "Huston: 'I Want to Keep Right on Going,'" *New York Times*, 11 December 1979, sec. C, p. 7.
6. From introduction to *Wise Blood*, quoted in publicity release of New Line Cinema.
7. Andrew Sarris, "Of Blood and Thunder and Despair," *Village Voice*, 25 February 1980.
8. Malcolm, "Huston," 7.
9. Aljean Harmetz, "Huston Filming 'Under the Volcano' beside Mist-Shrouded Popocatépetl," *New York Times*, 23 August 1983, sec. 3, p. 11.
10. Todd McCarthy, "Cracking the Volcano," *Film Comment*, July 1984, 60.
11. Pete Hamill, "Against All Odds," *American Film*, July-August 1984, 24.

Selected Bibliography

1. Books

Benayoun, Robert. *John Huston.* Paris: Editions Seghers, 1966. A studious film-by-film evaluation of Huston's work through the early 1960s.

Huston, John. *An Open Book.* New York: Alfred A. Knopf, 1980. The director's autobiography; thereby, the definitive source for all the adventure stories and anecdotes.

John Huston. [Washington, D.C.: American Film Institute], 1983. Illustrated program for the dinner at which Huston received the eleventh annual AFI Life Achievement Award, 3 March 1983, especially valuable for many photographs of Huston and scenes from his films.

Madsen, Axel. *John Huston.* Garden City, N.Y.: Doubleday & Co., 1978. A hastily and often sloppily written rehash of Huston stories.

Nolan, William F. *John Huston: King Rebel.* Los Angeles: Sherbourne Press, 1965. The first of the anecdotal biographies.

Pratley, Gerald. *The Cinema of John Huston.* New York: A. S. Barnes, 1977. An oral autobiography, transcribed and edited with plot summaries, film credits, and short comments interpolated.

Ross, Lillian. *Picture.* New York: Rinehart & Co., 1952. A minutely observed account, first published in the *New Yorker,* of the making of *The Red Badge of Courage* that accuses Huston of artistic irresponsibility.

Viertel, Peter. *White Hunter, Black Heart.* Garden City, N.Y.: Doubleday & Co., 1953. A fictionalized account of events surrounding the production of *The African Queen,* which portrays Huston as callous, headstrong, and obsessed with big game hunting.

2. Articles and Parts of Books

Agee, James. "Undirectable Director." In *Agee on Film.* New York: McDowell Obolensky, 1958, 319–31. Reprints from *Life* magazine (18 September 1950) the article that "canonized Huston prematurely."

Bachmann, Gideon. "How I Make Films: An Interview with John Huston." *Film Quarterly,* Fall 1965, 3–13. Huston responds articulately to intelligent questions.

Buache, Freddy. "John Huston." *Premier Plan* June 1966, 5–30. Film-by-film commentary by Buache and other European writers on every Huston work up to the date of publication.

Canby, Vincent. "Many Try, But *Wise Blood* Succeeds." *New York Times*, 2 March 1980, 2:19. An appreciation of Huston's power as an adapter from literature.

Godley, John. "John Huston." *Vogue*, 15 November 1955, 118–19-. A witty, firsthand account of the making of *Moby Dick*.

Greenberg, Peter S. "John Huston: The *Rolling Stone* Interview." *Rolling Stone*, 19 February 1981, 21-. Some comments on the films, mixed in with anecdotes and political musings.

Phillips, Gene D. "Talking with John Huston." *Film Comment*, May 1973, 15–19. An interview that sticks strictly to reflections on Huston's films.

Sarris, Andrew. "Johnny, We Finally Knew Ye." *Village Voice*, 19 May 1980. An overview of Huston's career by one of his most consistent detractors that is conciliatory in tone.

Taylor, John Russell. "John Huston and the Figure in the Carpet." *Sight and Sound*, Spring 1968, 70–72. A balanced look at Huston's work from the perspective of the release of *Reflections in a Golden Eye*.

Filmography

Commercial Feature Films directed by John Huston

THE MALTESE FALCON (Warner Brothers, 1941)
Producer: Hal Wallis
Screenplay: John Huston, from the novel by Dashiell Hammett
Director of photography: Arthur Edeson
Music: Adolph Deutsch
Editor: Thomas Richards
Cast: Humphrey Bogart (Sam Spade), Mary Astor (Brigid O'Shaughnessy),
Gladys George (Iva Archer), Peter Lorre (Joel Cairo), Sydney Greenstreet
(Casper Guttman), Jerome Cowan (Miles Archer), Elisha Cook, Jr. (Wilmer
Cook), Barton MacLane (Lt. Dundy), Ward Bond (Detective Polhaus),
Walter Huston (Captain Jacobi)
Running time: 100 minutes
New York opening: 3 October 1941

IN THIS OUR LIFE (Warner Brothers, 1942)
Producer: Hal Wallis
Screenplay: Howard Koch, from the novel by Ellen Glasgow.
Director of photography: Ernest Haller
Music: Max Steiner
Editor: William Holmes
Art direction by Robert Haas, with gowns by Orry-Kelly
Cast: Bette Davis (Stanley Timberlake), Olivia de Havilland (Roy), George
Brent (Craig Fleming), Dennis Morgan (Peter Kingsmill), Charles Coburn
(William Fleming), Frank Craven (Asa), Billie Burke (Lavinia), Hattie
McDaniel (maid)
Running time: 97 minutes
New York opening: 8 May 1942

ACROSS THE PACIFIC (Warner Brothers, 1942)
Producers: Jerry Wald and Jack Saper
Screenplay: Robert Macaulay, from the *Saturday Evening Post* serial "Aloha
Means Goodbye" by Robert Carson
Director of photography: Arthur Edeson
Music: Adolph Deutsch

Editor: Frank Magee
Special effects: Byron Haskin and Willard Van Enger
Cast: Humphrey Bogart (Rick Leland), Mary Astor (Alberta Marlow), Sydney Greenstreet (Dr. Lorenz), Victor Sen Yung (Joe Totsuiko)
Running time: 97 minutes
New York opening: 4 September 1942

THE TREASURE OF THE SIERRA MADRE (Warner Brothers, 1948)
Producer: Henry Blanke
Screenplay: John Huston, from the novel by B. Traven
Director of photography: Ted McCord
Music: Max Steiner
Editor: Owen Marks
Special effects: William McGann and H. F. Koenekamp
Cast: Humphrey Bogart (Fred Dobbs), Walter Huston (Howard), Tim Holt (Curtin), Barton MacLane (McCormick), Bobby Blake (Mexican Boy), John Huston (White Suit), Alfonso Bedoya (Gold Hat), Jack Holt (Flophouse Bum)
Running time: 126 minutes
New York opening: 23 January 1948
Academy Awards to John Huston for writing and directing and to Walter Huston as supporting actor

KEY LARGO (Warner Brothers, 1948)
Producer: Jerry Wald
Screenplay: John Huston and Richard Brooks, from the play by Maxwell Anderson
Director of photography: Karl Freund
Music: Max Steiner
Editor: Rudi Fehr
Special effects: William McGann and Robert Burks
Cast: Humphrey Bogart (Frank McCloud), Lauren Bacall (Norma Temple), Edward G. Robinson (Johnny Rocco), Lionel Barrymore (James Temple), Claire Trevor (Gaye Dawn), Monte Blue (Sheriff Ben Wade)
Running time: 101 minutes
New York opening: 16 June 1948

WE WERE STRANGERS (Horizon Productions/Columbia, 1949)
Producer: S. P. Eagle (Sam Spiegel).
Screenplay: John Huston and Robert Viertel, from an episode in the novel *Rough Sketch* by Robert Sylvester
Director of photography: Russell Merry
Music: George Antheil
Editor: Al Clark
Cast: Jennifer Jones (China Valdes), John Garfield (Tony Fenner), Pedro Armendariz (Armando Ariete), Gilbert Roland (Guillermo), Ramon Navarro (Chief), John Huston
Running time: 106 minutes
New York opening: 27 April 1949

THE ASPHALT JUNGLE (MGM, 1950)
Producer: Arthur Hornblow, Jr.
Screenplay: John Huston and Ben Meddow, from the novel by W. R.
Burnett
Director of photography: Harold Rosson
Music: Miklos Rosza
Editor: George Boemler
Cast: Sterling Hayden (Dix Handley), Louis Calhern (Alonzo D.
Emmerich), Jean Hagen (Doll Conovan), James Whitmore (Gus Minissi), Sam Jaffe
(Reimenschneider), Marilyn Monroe (girlfriend)
Running time: 105 minutes
New York opening: 8 June 1950

THE RED BADGE OF COURAGE (MGM, 1951)
Producer: Gottfried Reinhardt
Screenplay: John Huston, from the novel by Stephen Crane
Director of photography: Harold Rosson
Music: Bronislau Kaper
Editor: Ben Lewis
Cast: Audie Murphy (the Youth), Bill Mauldin (the Loud Soldier), Royal
Dano (the Tattered Soldier), Andy Devine (the Talkative Soldier), narration
by James Whitmore
Running time: 69 minutes
New York opening: 18 October 1951

THE AFRICAN QUEEN (Romulus-Horizon/United Artists, 1951)
Producer: S. P. Eagle
Screenplay: James Agee and John Huston, from the novel by C. S. Forester
Director of photography: Jack Cardiff, color by Technicolor
Music: Allan Gray
Editor: Ralph Kemplen
Katharine Hepburn's costumes by Doris Langley Moore
Cast: Katharine Hepburn (Rose Sayer), Humphrey Bogart (Charlie Allnutt),
Robert Morley (Brother Samuel Sayer), Peter Bull (German captain),
Theodore Bikel (German first officer)
Running time: 103 minutes
New York opening: 20 February 1952

MOULIN ROUGE (Romulus/United Artists 1953)
Producer: John Huston
Screenplay: Anthony Veiller and John Huston, from the novel by Pierre La
Mure
Director of photography: Oswald Morris, color by Technicolor
Music: Georges Auric
Editor: Ralph Kemplen
Costumes by Marcel Vertes
Cast: Jose Ferrer (Henri de Toulouse-Lautrec and his father), Colette
Marchand (Marie), Suzanne Flon (Myriamme), Zsa Zsa Gabor (Jane Avril),

Katherine Kath (La Goulue), Claude Nollier (Comtesse de Toulouse-Lautrec)
Running time: 120 minutes
New York opening: 10 February 1953

BEAT THE DEVIL (Romulus-Santana/United Artists, 1953)
Producer: John Huston, in association with Humphrey Bogart
Screenplay: John Huston and Truman Capote, from the novel by James Helvick
Director of photography: Oswald Morris
Music: Franco Mannino
Editor: Ralph Kemplen
Cast: Humphrey Bogart (Billy Dannreuther), Jennifer Jones (Gwendolen Chelm), Gina Lollabrigida (Maria Dannreuther), Robert Morley (Petersen), Peter Lorre (O'Hara)
Running time: 100 minutes
New York opening: 12 March 1953

MOBY DICK (A Moulin film, released by Warner Brothers, 1956)
Producer: John Huston
Screenplay: Ray Bradbury and John Huston, from the novel by Herman Melville
Director of photography: Oswald Morris, color by Technicolor
Music: Philip Stainton
Editor: Russell Lloyd
Special effects: Gus Lohman
Cast: Gregory Peck (Captain Ahab), Richard Basehart (Ishmael), Leo Genn (Starbuck), Harry Andrews (Stubb), Seamus Kelly (Flask), Philip Stainton (Bildad), Friedrich Ledebur (Queequeg), Tamba Alleney (Pip), Orson Welles (Father Marple), James Robertson Justice (Capt. Boomer)
Running time: 115 minutes
New York opening: 4 June 1956

HEAVEN KNOWS, MR. ALLISON (20th Century-Fox, 1957)
Producers: Buddy Adler and Eugene Frenke
Screenplay: John Huston and John Lee Mahin, from the novel by Charles Shaw
Director of photography: Oswald Morris, color by Technicolor
Music: Georges Auric
Editor: Russell Lloyd
Cast: Deborah Kerr (Sister Angela), Robert Mitchum (Mr. Allison)
Running time: 106 minutes
New York opening: 14 March 1957

THE BARBARIAN AND THE GEISHA (Twentieth Century-Fox, 1958)
Producer: Eugene Frenke
Screenplay: Charles Grayson, from the story by Ellis St. John
Director of photography: Charles G. Clarke, color by Eastmancolor
Music: Hugo Friedhofer

Editor: Stuart Gilmore
Cast: John Wayne (Townsend Harris), Eiko Ando (Okichi), Sam Jaffe (Henry
Heusken), So Yamomura (Tamura), Norman Thomson (Ship Captain)
Running time: 105 minutes
New York opening: 2 October 1958

THE ROOTS OF HEAVEN (Twentieth Century-Fox, 1958)
Producer: Darryl F. Zanuck
Screenplay: Romain Gary and Patrick Leigh-Fermor, from the novel by
Romain Gary
Director of photography: Oswald Morris, color by Eastmancolor
Music: Malcolm Arnold
Editor: Russell Lloyd
Cast: Trevor Howard (Morel), Juliette Greco (Minna), Errol Flynn
(Forsythe), Eddie Albert (Abe Fields), Orson Welles (Cy Segwick), Paul
Lukas (Saint-Denis), Herbert Lom (Orsini)
Running time: 125 minutes
New York opening: 15 October 1958

THE UNFORGIVEN (Continental/Hecht-Hill-Lancaster/United Artists,
1960)
Producer: James Hill
Screenplay: Ben Maddow, from the novel by Alan LeMay
Director of photography: Franz Planer, color by Technicolor
Music: Dimtri Tiomkin
Editor: Russell Lloyd
Cast: Audrey Hepburn (Rachel), Burt Lancaster (Ben Zachary), Audie
Murphy (Cash), Lillian Gish (Mattilda), Charles Bickford (Zeb Rawlins), John
Saxon (Johnny Portugal)
Running time: 125 minutes
New York opening: 6 April 1960

THE MISFITS (Seven Arts/United Artists, 1961)
Producer: Frank Taylor
Screenplay: Arthur Miller
Director of photography: Russell Metty
Music: Alex North
Editor: George Tomasini
Cast: Clark Gable (Gay Langland), Marilyn Monroe (Roslyn Taber),
Montgomery Clift (Perce Howland), Eli Wallach (Guido), Thelma Ritter
(Isabelle Steers), Kevin McCarthy (Raymond Taber), Estelle Winwood
(Church Lady)
Running time: 125 minutes
New York opening: 1 February 1961

FREUD: THE SECRET PASSION (Universal, 1962)
Producer: Wolfgang Reinhardt

Screenplay: Wolfgang Reinhardt and Charles Kaufman
Director of photography: Douglas Slocombe
Music: Jerry Goldsmith
Editor: Ralph Kemplen
Technical adviser: Earl A. Loomis, Jr.
Cast: Montgomery Clift (Sigmund Freud), Susannah York (Cecily Koertner),
Larry Parks (Dr. Joseph Breuer), Susan Kohner (Martha Freud), Erick
Portman (Dr. Theodore Meynert), prologue and epilogue read by John
Huston
Running time: 140 minutes
New York opening: 12 December 1962

THE LIST OF ADRIAN MESSENGER (Universal, 1963)
Producer: Edward Lewis
Screenplay: Anthony Veiller, from the novel by Phillip MacDonald
Director of photography: Joseph McDonald
Music: Jerry Goldsmith
Editors: Terry Morse, Hugh Fowler
Cast: George C. Scott (Anthony Gethyrn), Kirk Douglas (George Brougham),
Jacques Roux (Raoul Le Borg), Dana Wynter (Lady Jocelyn Bruttenholm),
Walter Tony Huston (Derek), Clive Brook (the Marquis of Gleneyre),
Herbert Marshall (Sir Wilfred Lucas), John Huston (Huntsman)
Guest stars: Robert Mitchum, Burt Lancaster, Frank Sinatra, Tony Curtis
Running time: 97 minutes
New York opening: 19 May 1963

THE NIGHT OF THE IGUANA (Seven Arts/MGM, 1964)
Producers: Ray Stark and John Huston
Screenplay: Anthony Veiller and John Huston, from the play by Tennessee
Williams
Director of photography: Gabriel Figueroa
Music: Benjamin Frankel
Editor: Ralph Kemplen
Cast: Richard Burton (Rev. Laurence Shannon), Ava Gardner (Maxine
Faulk), Deborah Kerr (Hannah Jelkes), Sue Lyon (Charlotte Goodall), James
Ward (Hank Prosner)
Running time: 118 minutes
New York opening: 31 May 1964

THE BIBLE . . . IN THE BEGINNING (20th Century-Fox, 1966)
Producer: Dino di Laurentiis
Screenplay: Christopher Fry
Director of photography: Giuseppe Rotunno, color by Technicolor (70 mm.)
Music: Toshiro Mayuzumi
Editor: Ralph Kemplen
Zoological consultant: Angelo Lombardi
Cast: Michael Parks (Adam), Ulla Bergyrd (Eve), Richard Harris (Cain),

Franco Nero (Abel), John Huston (Noah), Stephen Boyd (Nimrod), George
C. Scott (Abraham), Ava Gardner (Sarah), Peter O'Toole (the Three Angels),
Gabriele Ferzetti (Lot), Eleonora Rossi Drago (Lot's Wife), narrated by John
Huston
Running time: 175 minutes
New York opening: 28 September 1966

CASINO ROYALE (Columbia, 1967)
Producers: Charles K. Feldman and Jerry Bresler
Codirectors: Ken Hughes, Val Guest, Robert Parrish, Joseph McGrath
(Huston directed only the first sequence)
Screenplay: Wolf Mankowitz, John Law, and Michael Sayers, from the novel
by Ian Fleming
Director of photography: Jack Hildyard, color by Technicolor
Music: Burt Bacharach
Editor: Bill Lenny
Cast: (first sequence) David Niven (Sir James Bond), Deborah Kerr (Agent
Mimi), Peter Sellers, Orson Welles, Woody Allen, and many other stars
appear in later sequences
Running time: 131 minutes
New York opening: 28 April 1967

REFLECTIONS IN A GOLDEN EYE (Warner Brothers/ Seven Arts, 1967)
Producer: Ray Stark
Screenplay: Chapman Mortimer and Gladys Hill, from the novel by Carson
McCullers
Director of photography: Aldo Tonti
Music: Toshiro Mayuzumi
Editor: Russell Lloyd
Cast: Marlon Brando (Major Weldon Penderton), Elizabeth Taylor (Leonora
Penderton), Brian Keith (Lt. Col. Morris Langdon), Julie Harris (Alison
Langdon), Robert Forster (Private Williams)
Running time: 109 minutes
New York opening: 11 October 1967

SINFUL DAVEY (Mirisch Corporation/United Artists, 1969)
Producer: William N. Grof
Screenplay: James R. Webb, based on *The Life of David Haggart* by David
Haggart
Directors of photography: Ted Scaife and Freddie Young, color by
Eastmancolor
Music: Ken Thorne
Editor: Russell Lloyd
Cast: John Hurt (David Haggart), Pamela Franklin (Annie), Nigel Davenport
(Chief Constable Robertson), Ronald Fraser (MacNab), Robert Morley (Duke
of Argyll), Maxine Audley (Duchess of Argyle)
Running time: 95 minutes
New York opening: 4 June 1969

A WALK WITH LOVE AND DEATH (20th Century-Fox, 1969)
Producer: Carter DeHaven
Screenplay: Dale Wasserman, from the novel by Hans Koningsberger,
adapted for the screen by the author
Director of photography: Ted Scaife
Music: Georges Delerue
Editor: Russell Lloyd
Cast: Anjelica Huston (Claudia), Assaf Dyan (Heron of Foix), Anthony Corlan
(Robert), John Huston (Robert the Elder)
Running time: 90 minutes
New York opening: 5 October 1969

THE KREMLIN LETTER (20th Century-Fox, 1970)
Producers: Carter De Haven, Sam Wiesenthal
Screenplay: John Huston and Gladys Hill, from the novel by Noel Behn
Director of photography: Ted Scaife, in Panavision with color by DeLuxe
Music: Robert Drasnin
Editor: Russell Lloyd
Cast: Richard Boone (Ward), Bibi Andersson (Erika Boeck), Max von Sydow
(Col. Vladimir Kosnov), Patrick O'Neal (Lt. Commander Charles Rone),
George Sanders (The Warlock), Dean Jagger (The Highwayman), Lila
Kedrova (Madame Sophie), John Huston (Admiral)
Running time: 121 minutes
New York opening: 1 February 1970

FAT CITY (Rastar, released by Columbia, 1972)
Producer: Ray Stark
Screenplay: Leonard Gardner, from his novel
Director of photography: Conrad Hall, color by Eastmancolor
Music: "Help Me Make It Through the Night," written and sung by Kris
Kristofferson
Editor: Margaret Booth
Cast: Stacy Keach (Billy Tully), Jeff Bridges (Ernest Munger), Susan Tyrell
(Oma), Candy Clark (Faye), Curtis Cokes (Earl)
Running time: 96 minutes
New York opening: 26 July 1972

THE LIFE AND TIMES OF JUDGE ROY BEAN (National General, 1972)
Producer: John Foreman
Screenplay: John Milius
Director of photography: in Panavision, with color by Technicolor
Music: Maurice Jarre
Editor: Hugh S. Fowler
Cast: Paul Newman (Judge Roy Bean), Jacqueline Bisset (Rose Bean), Ava
Gardner (Lily Langtry), Tab Hunter (Sam Dodd), John Huston (Grizzly
Adams), Stacy Keach (Bad Bob), Roddy McDowell (Frank Gass), Anthony
Perkins (Reverend LaSalle), Victoria Principal (Maria Elena)
Running time: 124 minutes
New York opening: 18 December 1972

THE MACKINTOSH MAN (Warner Brothers, 1973)
Producer: John Foreman
Screenplay: Walter Hill, from the novel *The Freedom Trap* by Desmond
Bagley
Director of photography: Oswald Morris
Music: Maurice Jarre
Editor: Russell Lloyd
Cast: Paul Newman (Joseph Rearden), Dominique Sanda (Mrs. Smith),
James Mason (Sir George Wheeler), Harry Andrews (Angus Mackintosh)
Running time: 99 minutes
New York opening: 25 July 1973

THE MAN WHO WOULD BE KING (Allied Artists, 1975)
Producer: John Foreman
Screenplay: John Huston and Gladys Hill, from the short story by Rudyard
Kipling
Director of photography: Oswald Morris, color by Eastmancolor
Music: Maurice Jarre
Special effects: Dick Parker
Editor: Russell Lloyd
Cast: Sean Connery (Daniel Dravot), Michael Caine (Peachy Carnahan),
Christopher Plummer (Rudyard Kipling)
Running time: 132 minutes
New York opening: 17 December 1975

WISE BLOOD (New Line Cinema, 1979)
Producers: Michael and Kathy Fitzgerald
Screenplay: Benedict Fitzgerald, from the novel by Flannery O'Connor
Director of photography: Gerald Fisher
Music: Alex North
Editor: Robert Silvi
Cast: Brad Dourif (Hazel Motes), Ned Beatty (Hoover Shoates), Harry Dean
Stanton (Asa Hawks), Daniel Shor (Enoch Emery), Amy Wright (Sabbath
Lily), Mary Neil Santacroce (Landlady), John Huston (Grandfather)
Running time: 108 minutes
American premiere at the seventeenth New York Film Festival, Alice Tully
Hall, 29 September 1979. Commercial New York opening, 16 February 1980

PHOBIA (Paramount, 1980)
Producers: Larry Spiegel, Mel Bergman
Screenplay: Ronald Shusett, Gary Sherman, Lew Lehman, James Sangster,
and Peter Bellwood
Director of photography: Reginald Morris
Cast: Paul Michael Glaser, John Colicos, Susan Hogan, Alexandra Stewart,
Lisa Langlois
Note: This film was made in Canada and has never been theatrically
distributed in the United States. No further information about it is available.

VICTORY (Lorimar/Paramount, 1981)
Producer: Freddie Fields
Screenplay: Evan Jones and Yabo Yablonsky, from a short story by Yablonsky,
Djordje Milicevic, and Jeff Maguire
Director of photography: Gerry Fisher
Music: Bill Conti
Editor: Roberto Silvi
Cast: Sylvester Stallone (Robert Hatch), Michael Caine (John Colby), Pele
(Luis Fernandez), Max von Sydow (Major Karl von Steiner)
Running time: 110 minutes
New York opening: 31 July 1981

ANNIE (Rastar/Columbia, 1982)
Producer: Ray Stark
Screenplay: Carol Sobieski, from the Broadway musical by Thomas Meehan,
based on the comic strip by Harold Gray
Director of photography: Richard Moore
Music: Charles Strouse, with lyrics by Martin Charnin
Musical staging and choreography: Arlene Phillips
Editor: Michael A. Stevenson
Cast: Aileen Quinn (Annie), Albert Finney (Daddy Warbucks), Carol Burnett
(Miss Hannigan), Bernadette Peters (Lily), Tim Currie (Rooster), Anne
Reineking (Grace Farrell), Geoffrey Holder (Punjab), Roger Minami (Asp),
Edward Herrmann (President Franklin D. Roosevelt), Lois DeBanzie
(Eleanor Roosevelt)
Running time: 128 minutes
New York opening: 21 May 1982

UNDER THE VOLCANO (Universal, 1984)
Producer: Michael Fitzgerald
Screenplay: Guy Gallo, based on the novel by Malcolm Lowry
Photography: Gabriel Figueroa
Art direction: Gunther Gerzso
Music: Alex North
Cast: Albert Finney (the Consul), Jacqueline Bissett (Yvonne), Anthony
Andrews (Hugh)
Running time: 110 minutes
New York opening: 13 June 1984

Government Documentaries

REPORT FROM THE ALEUTIANS (United States Signal Corps, 1943)
Screenplay: John Huston
Photographers: Capt. Ray Scott, Lt. Jules Buck, Sgt. Freeman C. Collins,
Cpl. Buzz Ellsworth, Cpl. Herman Crabtrey
Musical score: Dimitri Tiomkin
Narration by John Huston and Walter Huston

Running time: 45 minutes
Distributed by M-G-M for the War Activities Committee

SAN PIETRO (THE BATTLE OF SAN PIETRO) (United States Signal
Corps, 1944)
Screenplay: John Huston
Photographers: John Huston, Lt. Jules Buck and cameramen of the United
States Signal Corps
Narration by John Huston
Running time: 32 minutes
New York opening: 11 June 1945

LET THERE BE LIGHT (United States Signal Corps, 1946, released in
1981)
Screenplay: Charles Kaufman and John Huston
Photographers: John Huston, Stanley Cortez
Music by Dimitri Tiomkin
Narration by Walter Huston
Running time: 59 minutes
Never officially opened by Signal Corps

INDEPENDENCE (National Parks Service/Twentieth Century-Fox, 1975)
Producers: Joyce and Lloyd Ritter
Screenplay: Joyce and Lloyd Ritter, with Thomas McGrath
Historical consultant: L. H. Butterfield
Director of photography: Owen Roizman, in Panavision, color by
Eastmancolor
Art director: Stephen Grimes
Costumes: Ann Roth
Cast: William Atherton (Benjamin Rush), Pat Hingle (John Adams), Ken
Howard (Thomas Jefferson), Anne Jackson (Abigail Adams), Patrick O'Neal
(George Washington), Paul Sparer (John Hancock), Eli Wallach (Benjamin
Franklin)
Running time: 28 minutes
Note: This pseudodocumentary is shown daily at Independence Hall
National Park in Philadelphia. Showings are planned until the end of the
century.

Filmscripts by John Huston

1931   *A House Divided* (Universal, directed by William Wyler)

1932   *Murders in the Rue Morgue* (Universal, directed by Robert Florey)
       Law and Order (Universal, directed by Edward L. Cahn)

1938   *Jezebel* (Warner Brothers, directed by William Wyler)
       The Amazing Dr. Clitterhouse (Warner Brothers, directed by Anatole
       Litvak)

1939   *Juarez* (Warner Brothers, directed by William Dieterle)

1940   *Dr. Ehrlich's Magic Bullet* (Warner Brothers, directed by William Dieterle)

1941   *High Sierra* (Warner Brothers, directed by Raoul Walsh)
        Sergeant York (Warner Brothers, directed by Howard Hawks)

1946   *Three Strangers* (Warner Brothers, directed by Jean Negulesco)

Performances in Films by John Huston

1929   *Two Americans* (Paramount-Famous-Players-Lasky, directed by John Meehan, and starring Walter Huston)

John Huston has played roles or delivered narrations in many of the films that he has directed, beginning with *Freud* (1962). See also the credits in Part I for *The List of Adrian Messenger, The Bible, A Walk with Love and Death, The Kremlin Letter, The Life and Times of Judge Roy Bean,* and *Wise Blood.* He has also appeared since 1963 in these films directed by others:

1963   *The Cardinal* (Columbia, directed by Otto Preminger)

1968   *Candy* (Cinerama Releasing Corporation, directed by Christian Marquand)

1969   *De Sade* (CCC/Trans-Continental/American International, directed by Cy Enfield)

1970   *Myra Breckinridge* (Twentieth Century-Fox, directed by Michael Sarne)
        The Bridge in the Jungle (Sagittarius/Capricorn, directed by Pancho Kohner)

1971   *The Deserter* (De Laurentiis/Paramount, directed by Burt Kennedy)
        Man in the Wilderness (Warner Brothers, directed by Richard Sarafian)

1973   *Battle for the Planet of the Apes* (Twentieth Century-Fox, directed by J. Lee Thompson)

1974   *Chinatown* (Paramount, directed by Roman Polanski)

1975   *Breakout* (Columbia, directed by Tom Gries)
        The Wind and the Lion (M-G-M/United Artists, directed by John Milius)

1976   *Sherlock Holmes in New York* (Twentieth Century-Fox Television/ NBC-TV, directed by Boris Sagal)
        Circasia (an independent film produced by Kevin McClory)

1977   *Tentacles* (American International, directed by Oliver Hellman)
        The Rhinemann Exchange (NBC-TV, directed by Burt Kennedy)
        Hollywood on Trial (documentary produced by James Gutman and directed by David Halpern, Jr.)
        The Hobbit (Rankin-Bass Productions/NBC-TV, animation produced and directed by Arthur Rankin, Jr., and Jules Bass)

1978   *The Word* (CBS-TV, directed by Richard Lang)

El Triangulo diabolico de las Bermudas (The Bermuda Triangle) (Conacine/Nucleo, directed by Rene Cardona, Jr.)
Angela (Zev Braun Productions, directed by Boris Sagal)

1979   *Jaguar Lives* (American International, directed by Ernest Pintoff)
       Winter Kills (AVCO Embassy, directed by William Richert)
       The Battle of Mareth/The Greatest Battle (Titanus/Dimension, directed by Hank Milestone)
       Head On (Michael Grant Productions, directed by Michael Grant)

1980   *John Huston's Dublin* (documentary produced and directed by John McGreevy)
       Agee (Documentary produced and directed by Ross Spears)
       The Visitor (International Picture Show Co., directed by Michael J. Paradise)

1982   *Cannery Row* (MGM/United Artists, directed by David S. Ward)

1983   *Lovesick* (Ladd Company/Warner Brothers, directed by Marshall Brickman)
       A Minor Miracle (an independent production by Tom Moyer, directed by Terry Tannen)

Films about John Huston

The Life and Times of John Huston, Esq. (Allan King and Associates, NET/BBC/CBC, 1966). Producer and director: Roger Graef. Cast: John Huston, Anjelica Huston, Tony Huston, Gladys Hill, Evelyn Keyes, Elizabeth Taylor, Marlon Brando, Burl Ives.

John Huston: A War Remembered (KCET-TV, Los Angeles/Rastar Television, 1981). Producer/Directer: Jim Washburn. Cast: John Huston and Clere Roberts, discussing Huston's wartime documentaries for the United States Army Signal Corps.

Lights! Camera! Annie! (KCET-TV, Los Angeles, Kaleidoscope Films, Columbia/Rastar, 1982). Producers: Margery Doppelt, Gregory McClatchy. Director: Andrew J. Kuehn. Cast: John Huston, Ray Stark, Aileen Quinn, Albert Finney, Carol Burnett, Tim Curry, Bernadette Peters.

The Directors Guild Series: John Huston (Maddox-Turrow Productions, 1982). Producer: Randolph Turrow. Director: William Crain. Cast: John Huston, Phillip Dunne.

Index